It's No ~~There's~~

Money

in PODIATRY

A Podiatrists' Guide to Earning
More, Working Less and Enjoying
What You Do Each Day

Tyson E. Franklin

TESTIMONIALS

"As a consultant within the franchise industry I have met plenty of business owners and entrepreneurs, and after meeting Tyson I unexpectedly ended up learning more about business and how to operate a business more efficiently. Tyson has an outstanding attitude and outlook towards business, and like the old saying goes, 'if you want to be successful, hang around or learn from successful people', and Tyson certainly fits this description."

Len Ferguson (Finn Franchise Brokers)

"I would not be in the financial position I am today if it wasn't for Tyson's experience, knowledge and encouragement. He helped guide me through the whole process when I opened my podiatry clinic in Townsville, and whenever I came up with grand business ideas he would offer constructive advice, even if there were no financial benefits in it for him; instead his advice has always centred around what was best for me. Tyson is a great mentor and friend."

Hayley Paterson (Foundation Podiatry, Townsville)

"Tyson Franklin is an innovative business owner and you can guarantee this book will provide fantastic business advice for anyone in the Health Industry, not just podiatry."

Tom Maher (Owner, Cairns Total Physiotherapy)

"Tyson is a dynamo! He has an amazing energy, an all-action attitude and tries just about everything in business at least once. Every business can learn from his successes, not just health professionals."

Nicky Jurd (author and business owner, Precedence.com.au)

"Tyson Franklin definitely walks his talk, having built his own successful podiatry business which has given him the lifestyle that every courageous entrepreneur deserves. He is certainly the authority on how to unlock the potential of a podiatry business. This book will be a must-read if you want to achieve that same full potential in your podiatry business."

Sam Harrop (author of Getting Stuff Done*)*

"Strategic, charismatic, creative and seriously funny…working with Tyson is a laugh a minute and his ideas are kick ass."

Troy Haines (theSPACE Startup & Innovation Coach)

ACKNOWLEDGEMENTS

I'm competitive by nature; it's in my DNA, and if it wasn't for my older brother Tony Franklin heading off to university I may never have gone myself. *If he can do it, then I can do it* was always my attitude, so I thank him for creating an educational path for me to follow. He has unknowingly inspired me my whole life, but let's keep that a secret.

To write this book I woke up most mornings about 4 am for six months. At 4 am you need coffee, and to my knowledge they have not yet invented a coffee machine that has stealth capabilities, so unbeknown to me I woke my wife and daughter most mornings, but they never once complained, and for this I cannot thank them enough. My wife Christine and my daughter Tia have supported and encouraged me throughout this whole writing process. It was amazing and I'm truly grateful; thank you, thank you, thank you.

And finally to my son Tyson Jr, who has started studying Podiatry at Newcastle University in NSW. It honours me to think he wants to follow in my footsteps.

DEDICATION

I dedicate this book to Brian Franklin, my father, who passed away in 1983 and never got the chance to see how much his two sons achieved. I'm sure he would be proud of us both.

First Published in Australia in 2014 by
Proarch Franchising Pty Ltd
PO Box 39E
Earlville Qld 4870

National Library of Australia Cataloguing-in-Publication entry:

Author:	Franklin, Tyson E.
Title:	It's no secret...there's money in podiatry: a podiatrists' guide to earning more, working less and enjoying what you do each day
ISBN:	9780992557904 (paperback)
	9780992557911 (ebook: epub)
	9780992557928 (ebook: Kindle)
Subjects:	Podiatry – Economic aspects.
	Success in business.
Dewey Number:	650.1

Cover design by Peter Reardon, Pipeline Design
Internal design by Michael Hanrahan Publishing
Printed in Australia by McPherson's Printing

Disclaimer

The material in this publication is of the nature of general comment only, and
does not represent professional advice. It is not intended to provide specific
guidance for particular circumstances and it should not be relied on as the basis
for any decision to take action or not take action on any matter which it covers.
Readers should obtain professional advice where appropriate, before making any
such decision. To the maximum extent permitted by law, the author and publisher
disclaim all responsibility and liability to any person, arising directly or indirectly
from any person taking or not taking action based on the information in this
publication.

CONTENTS

INTRODUCTION

It's no secret, there's money in podiatry – in fact, there's *a lot* of money in podiatry, and if anyone tells you otherwise they're lying. Every Podiatrist should be earning a healthy six-figure income. Well, actually I should rephrase that: every Podiatrist who is self-employed should be earning a healthy six-figure income, and if not, they're doing something wrong. Being an exceptional Podiatrist does not give you a right of passage to business success. This is an additional skill that must be acquired.

> **"You've baked a really lovely cake, but then you've covered it in dog sh#t."**
>
> Steve Jobs

This quote by Steve Jobs is quite funny, but unfortunately it does sum up many podiatry businesses. The practitioner has all the required skills, there's no doubt, and they have invested a ton of money in having the latest equipment, which they know how to use. *Basically they have baked a really lovely cake* and then, without any business knowledge, marketing plan, or systems in place, they open their doors for business, resulting in...you guessed it...a cake covered in dog sh#t. But it doesn't need to be this way.

We all know that a layperson in the street cannot simply decide they want to be a Podiatrist and start doing toenail surgery the following week; that would be ridiculous – *and criminal.* It takes years of training to become a proficient Podiatrist, so it makes sense that if you want to have a successful podiatry business, earning six figures, you need to also be prepared to dedicate an adequate amount of time to acquire these new skills, and become a proficient business owner.

I've always had an interest in business, which is why I was reading *Making Money Made Simple*, by Noel Whittaker, in my spare time and not *Common Foot Disorders*, by Neale. Did this mean I cared more about making money than treating my future patients? No, not at all, but I knew if I was going to work for myself one day and have a successful podiatry business, I had to learn more about business and how it related back to my profession. University is a great place to learn about podiatry, but a terrible place to learn about running your own business. University does not prepare you for self-employment; it merely prepares you to be a competent employee, so if you're serious about owning your own podiatry business and earning a healthy six-figure income, you need to be prepared to understand the fundamentals of business.

I believe everyone deep down wants to be successful because the opposite of success is failure, and no one wants to be a failure, however only a small percentage of people are prepared to do what's necessary to achieve success. I once read that if you took all the wealth in the world and divided it equally among everyone, in five years' time the rich would be rich, the middle class would be middle class and the poor would be *complaining about all the rich bastards that ripped them off and stole all their money.*

The truth of the matter is, if you never learn how to make money, you'll never keep it. The rich would become rich again, not because they ripped off the poor, but because they know what it takes to become rich again and also how to do it. I've established many profitable podiatry businesses over the past 25 years, and if it was all taken away from me tomorrow, within 12 months I would rebuild because I know exactly what to do. Business success doesn't occur by osmosis, it's a learned skill and it's a skill you need to master, just like you did with your podiatry skills – and together I think this can be achieved.

I would like to point out that I didn't go to an expensive private school, instead I went to one of those public schools you read about in the papers – for all the wrong reasons. However, my school did have some good attributes that many are unaware of. In one particular year my school held the record for the highest teenage pregnancy rate and also had one of the best football teams in the Brisbane district, so if you were male it was a great school. Seriously though, where you come from is not a predetermining factor of future success, it's where you see yourself going that's important. Having a private school education is no guarantee of success and – accordingly – going to a public school with a bad reputation is no excuse for failure.

If you're just starting out in business, or seriously considering it, I would highly recommend finding yourself a podiatry mentor, someone you can talk with on a regular basis, because working for yourself can be a very lonely place. Just make sure they have experience in podiatry business ownership. It's also important to attend state and national podiatry conferences, because you want to connect with other entrepreneurial Podiatrists. I'm not sure how this happens, because there's no secret handshake that I'm aware of, but Podiatrists with that entrepreneurial spirit seem to gravitate towards each other. You need to find them and hang out with them, because this is how you learn.

By the time you turn the last page of this book, I want you to have the confidence and belief that you too can own a great podiatry business and be making a healthy six-figure income in the next few years, year after year. If you've been in business for some time and you're already making good money, I hope after reading this book you're making even more, because if you're prepared to do the work then you deserve all the prosperity that comes with it.

Let's get started!
Tyson E. Franklin

PART I
BUSINESS

1
MOVING OUT OF YOUR COMFORT ZONE

Years ago, if someone had told me I'd be living in Cairns one day I would have laughed. Why would I leave the Gold Coast? It was my home and where I felt safe and comfortable…but here I am now in tropical North Queensland, and loving it.

My first podiatry business was on the Gold Coast, and it wasn't too successful. After four years I was making a living and that was about it. I had no business skills and my marketing consisted of placing an ad in the newspaper and phone directory, and putting up cheap signage. The thought of one day having a podiatry business that made hundreds of thousands of dollars profit each year never crossed my mind; back then I just wanted to pay the bills. Fortunately, after four years I recalled some advice given to me by Alan Crawford, Head of the Podiatry School at QUT: he said if he was going to set up a podiatry clinic he would move to a regional area. To be more specific, he said he would move to Cairns because it needed another Podiatrist, so I took his advice, sold my podiatry business on the Gold Coast and moved to Cairns in 1992.

My podiatry business in Cairns was a financial success from day one, even though my business knowledge had not changed, which goes to show that *any idiot can open a podiatry business and make good money if they open it in the right location – I was living proof.* So there's the contrast between staying in my comfort zone on the Gold Coast – where I made little money – and moving to Cairns, which was way outside my comfort zone, but I made good money right from the beginning.

Now don't get me wrong, I'm not saying that the Gold Coast was a terrible place to set up a podiatry business, because I know of other podiatrists that set up business after me and financially did quite well, but for me, at that particular point in my career, it was not a good place for me to be...*I was far too comfortable*, and I needed to move away so I could grow as a business person.

> **"Experience tells you what to do;
> confidence allows you to do it."**
>
> Stan Smith

I know many Podiatrists who make just enough money to keep them in the profession, but not quite enough to really enjoy life, take their family on regular holidays or do the other things they really want to do. As BCF would say, *"That's not living".* Experience is telling them to make changes, but their lack of confidence won't allow them to. Instead they will do nothing and over the next few decades, *yes decades*, they will make a few dollars – just enough to get by – and eventually retire. Often these Podiatrists become bitter and twisted towards their colleagues who have done well financially, and will often say they must be breaking the rules.

So what are *your plans*? Are you planning to stay where you grew up and where you live now, possibly in *your* comfort zone, or are you prepared to move and live somewhere else? Are you going to open your podiatry business in an area that you're familiar with, or will you live on the edge and move outside your comfort zone? If you've been in business for a few years already and it's not performing as well as you'd like, then maybe you should be asking yourself the same questions?

Because it's only when you move out of your comfort zone that amazing things happen.

Moving out of your comfort zone though doesn't necessarily mean you have to relocate to another city as I did, it may simply mean you need to relocate your existing business to a better location.

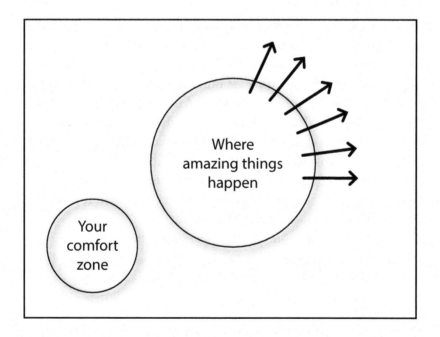

"Confidence is contagious; so is lack of confidence."

Vince Lombardi

CHOOSING THE RIGHT LOCATION

As a general rule, *the better the location, the higher the rent*, therefore it's unlikely your first business will be on a main road, so the next best thing is to find a road that is very familiar to everyone. If you're new to the area, simply ask people to name three connecting roads that are popular. If you're told the same connecting road multiple times then that should be the first area you investigate, however your budget is still going to determine your exact location.

Short-term thinking

Never think that your first location is going to be your last location and that you cannot move. Your podiatry business can be relocated every few years if extra space is required, which is why I suggest taking a short-term lease initially – only two or three years – and also looking for a premises that requires very little fit out, because when you leave you cannot take the fit out with you.

The term of your lease will also be affected by any financing arrangements you have in place. If you take out a five-year loan with a finance company they will want the term of the lease to be at least five years, to match your repayments. However, if you have no finance you can do whatever you want.

These have been some of my moves over the years:

- My first podiatry business in Cairns was approximately 60 m² and I spent nothing on the fit out because it was already in place. *Perfect!*

- My current location, which was my fifth move over a 21-year period, is on the busiest road in Cairns, is 210 m², and I spent a lot on the fit out, however my wife and I own the building so the fit out is ours to keep, so once again, *perfect!*

- When I established Proarch Podiatry Mackay, I took out a two-year lease and the location was approximately 50 m². The fit out was minimal because it was small, and by keeping our overheads to a minimum we made a profit from the first month, which was…you guessed it…*perfect!*

It's rare, but I've seen Podiatrists go bankrupt because they had visions of grandeur and their first location was far too large for their initial needs, which meant they had to over-borrow. *That's not perfect, that's stupid!*

SO WHAT MAKES A GOOD LOCATION?

Be easy to find

There is nothing more annoying than driving up and down a street looking for a business, especially if you're running late. Make sure your podiatry business is located near a distinguishable landmark or business that you can leverage from. "We're located next to the business with the large red car on the roof," is far easier than saying, "We're located at 3939 Elm Street".

Have easy parking

The second most annoying thing after not being able to find a business is finding it and then not being able to find a car park within walking distance. A patient may drive around in circles looking for a car park the first time, but they won't continue to do this if there are other options available to them – meaning a Podiatrist with better parking.

Have good signage

Regardless of your location, there needs to be an area where you can place some good signage, and if it can be illuminated at night that's even better. My business on the Gold Coast had very poor signage opportunities, which probably contributed to its poor performance. In addition to this, it was positioned partly in a garden bed, which meant every three months I had to trim a few hedges, otherwise it could not be seen.

Have a good tenant mix

The tenant mix can be a location winner or a location killer. If you're looking at a premises in a small complex with mixed tenancies, consider who your neighbours are going to be. Having other health professionals or service businesses can be a positive, however being located between a tattoo parlour and a drug rehab centre may not be. You cannot guarantee who your neighbours will be in the future, but the current tenant mix is a good indication.

Stay at eye level

Your location should also take into account the age and agility of your future patients. Will your business be located on the ground floor or will it be on the first floor? Being on the ground floor makes for easier access and is much easier to find and see from the street. If you're considering the first floor of a building, is there an elevator, or only steps?

I remember a friend who had a clinic for approximately 10 years, and over this time he had developed a considerable number of elderly patients. This was never his intention, so without thinking it through completely, he relocated his clinic to the first floor of the same building, meaning patients had to walk up 25 steps to reach his front entrance. His goal was to reduce the number of older patients being able to reach his clinic, which he achieved, however his overall patient numbers also dropped significantly. He failed to consider the following when relocating upstairs:

- He lost his eye-catching street-level visibility, meaning people walking past didn't know he was there.

- He lost his signage positioning because it went to the new tenants who moved into his old position.

- People with painful feet don't want to walk up 25 steps.

But the biggest killer, which he never considered, was a smart Podiatrist noticed the relocation upstairs, so they opened across the road, at street level, directly opposite his old location. They did very well. This new Podiatrist was in a far better position and they picked up all the walking-by foot traffic, and in addition to this they immediately attracted all of his elderly patients that could not walk up 25 steps. It took more than two years for him to recover, and eventually he moved his business back to street level.

DON'T BE AFRAID TO TAKE ON THE BIG CLINICS

Most Podiatrists would avoid opening their business in a town or suburb where a large podiatry business already exists, especially if it employs multiple Podiatrists, however I think it's something worth considering. If one podiatry business can employ multiple Podiatrists, doesn't this tell you there's a lot of podiatry work available in that particular area? Before taking on a large clinic though you need to do your homework. You can't just open next door and attack them head on, instead you need to study them:

- What are their strengths and weaknesses?

- What are they known for?

- What is their current marketing strategy?

- Where do they advertise?

- What services do they offer?

Once you've gathered this information, only then should you consider opening in opposition.

When I helped Hayley Paterson open her podiatry business in Townsville this is what she faced:

- There were four well-established Podiatry businesses.

- Two had been established for well over 20 years.

- Two owners had previously worked as tutors at the Podiatry School.

- All four businesses had reputable owners.

- One owner was on the Queensland Podiatry Board.

- Another owner was the President of the Queensland Podiatry Association.

- Another was on the Podiatry Council.

- One was a Fellow of the Australasian Academy of Podiatric Sports Medicine.

- Two clinics employed multiple Podiatrists.

- All had very professional-looking businesses.

- Both Townsville national sporting teams (rugby league and basketball) were already linked with one clinic.

- The Army Base was closely linked to another clinic.

Based on the above information you would have to be brave to open another podiatry business in Townsville, but that is exactly what Hayley did, and with some assistance she has gone on to create a very profitable business.

Was Hayley a naturally gifted businessperson? I would have to say no, because when Hayley worked with me in Cairns she was a new graduate and had no business knowledge, however she was willing to learn. She was also prepared to put in the work required to have a successful podiatry business and she was very conservative how she spent her money, and now she deserves all the accolades that come her way. So never be afraid to take on the big clinics; in fact, use it as motivation.

It's No Secret, There's Money In Podiatry, however…you need to venture outside of your comfort zone.

DO YOU REALLY NEED SATELLITE CLINICS?

Many Podiatrists starting out in business want to look and feel much larger than they really are, and to accomplish this they want to work from three or four locations on different days of the week. Is starting your business this way a good idea or bad idea? Well, this depends on your long-term goals and the type of podiatry business you want to have one day, however before you consider opening a satellite practice I think you need to understand what a satellite practice is…and what it is not.

By definition, *a satellite is an outpost or an object that orbits around or is dependent upon a much larger stationary object.* This is where some Podiatrists get the whole concept of satellite clinics wrong: they never actually have one larger, stationary podiatry business with satellite clinics orbiting. Instead, they have multiple clinics that they work at on different days of the week, therefore by definition they are not satellite practices at all; what they have are multiple part-time podiatry clinics separated by distance.

Satellite practices can be a good business move, especially if an area is not being serviced by another podiatry business and you're positive there is huge potential. However, before committing yourself to a satellite practice you should consider:

- the amount of time and effort required to set it up correctly

- the costs involved in setting up a professional satellite location

- the amount of time you'll be away from your main practice, where you are already paying rent – this is especially important if you are a sole practitioner

- travel time, both there and back.

If your main reason for setting up a satellite practice is that the main practice is not busy enough, I would suggest you're doing it for the wrong reason and you need to put more time and effort into building your main practice. Calculating your cost-to-benefit ratio should help you decide if a satellite practice is a great business decision or not.

I have had many satellite podiatry clinics over the years, some very profitable and others not so good, and at the time of writing this particular book I have none. Instead I have one very profitable, large, stationary podiatry clinic and shoe store which is very successful and makes great profits, and more importantly gives me a lot of time with my family. This does not mean I will not consider opening another satellite clinic in the future, however knowing what I know now I would do it differently.

If you're seriously thinking about opening a satellite clinic, in addition to the above considerations, also give some thought to:

- The location: will you have your own premises or will it be located within another business, such as a doctors or physiotherapy clinic?

- If it's located within another business, do you have exclusive use of the room so supplies and equipment can be left on site, or are you required to pack and unpack every time you visit?

- What type of examination bench will you be working from? This is especially important for your own posture and the safety of your patients.

- Is there adequate lighting?

- Who is looking after and servicing the main business while the satellite clinic is being serviced? Have you got other staff?

- How much is it going to cost you to establish a professional satellite clinic?

There are really only three reasons for establishing a satellite practice:

Reason 1: You want to reach patients who would otherwise not use your services because of distance.

Reason 2: To create additional work for a new Podiatrist commencing employment.

Reason 3: To make more money.

If there is sufficient evidence that you need to open a satellite practice then you should do it...*but* do it professionally or not at all.

*After reading this chapter, what ideas are going through your head? Write them down **right now**.*

_____

_____

_____

_____

_____

_____

_____

_____

2

ADVISORS, INSURANCE, MONEY AND EQUIPMENT

ADVISORS

To have a successful podiatry business you're going to need some expert advisors along the way, especially when it comes to financial and legal matters, therefore you need a good lawyer and a good accountant. Your lawyer will assist you with contracts in relation to financing, equipment leases and renting premises, whereas your accountant will be required to ensure your business is structured correctly. For example, will you be a sole trader or a company? Do you require a family trust? These are very important decisions, which is why you need a lawyer and accountant immediately to help you with this.

I would also highly recommend getting a bookkeeper. You may find your accountant has a bookkeeper onsite; if not, ask for a recommendation. A bookkeeper will help you set up your financial records properly and will keep them in order. They will prepare your monthly profit & loss statements, prepare income activity statements, business activity statements, and also calculate your superannuation guarantee amounts. Even if you have no staff, you still must pay superannuation for yourself if you operate as a company. My bookkeeper also does my fortnightly wages, therefore calculating the amount of tax to deduct and accumulated holidays for my full-time staff members. An important point to note: your bookkeeper charges far less than your accountant, so not only do they save you time, they also save you money. If you walk into your accountant's office with a shoebox full of receipts at the end of each financial year you will pay for your laziness, whereas if you have a bookkeeper you will provide your accountant with an electronic file containing all your financial information.

You'll get what you pay for, so never select an advisor based on price. Think about it; are there any cheap Podiatrists in your area? What's your opinion of them? Are they any good? It's always a good idea to ask friends and family who they use for legal and financial advice and then ask why they use these particular advisors. You want intelligent answers. If you have good advisors already then that's good news, however if you're not happy with them, change! I've had four accountants in my lifetime and I've had my current accountant for 10-plus years. What's important is you find advisors you're comfortable with and you trust; your advisors are going to know everything about you and your business, so trust is paramount.

INSURANCE

Next, you need to get your insurances in order. Some insurance cannot be avoided, such as professional indemnity insurance, however it is tax deductible. If you have an employee, even for a few hours per week, you must have a Work Cover policy. You need to do this immediately because if an injury occurs at work, or under some circumstances travelling to or from work, you may be held liable. Work Cover only protects employees, it does not insure the business owner. Therefore, depending on your circumstances and commitments, you should consider income protection and business expense insurance as well. I used to think income protection insurance was a waste of money, especially when I was young and bulletproof. But when I was 24 I could not work for almost two years due to a hand problem, so I'm glad the insurance salesmen diligently pursued me.

If you've borrowed money to finance your podiatry business, you may be asked by the financier to take out life insurance to cover the debt if anything happens to you, unless you have personal security or a guarantor.

With all agreements, especially insurance, always carefully read the terms and conditions. Make sure you write down on a separate piece of paper anything an insurance agent says to you during your meetings that does not appear in the contract. Date it and have them sign it before they leave. If they will not sign it, you need to find another insurance agent who is going to be straight with you.

When you add it all up, insurance is not cheap and many new business owners fail to take all their insurance premiums into account when they are preparing their budgets and cash flow. These additional costs can stifle your entrepreneurial spirit if you're not prepared.

> "There are worse things in life than death. Have you ever spent an evening with an insurance salesman?"
>
> Woody Allen

CASH IS KING

Many podiatry businesses struggle in their first few years because they've gone into the venture full of enthusiasm and then quickly run out of money. If you're considering opening a podiatry business right now, you should have enough cash in your bank account to cover all your business expenses for a minimum of three months. Anything less than that and you're kidding yourself. Lack of funds can be very stressful, and stress affects your judgment and decision-making capabilities. You want to build your business with a clear head, not a cloudy head concerned with paying next month's rent. Good cash flow allows you to pay all your accounts on time and also gives you the ability to purchase in bulk and make significant savings, especially on items you use on a regular basis. You will also save money on freight if you're ordering fewer times throughout the year.

Don't rush into opening a clinic if you don't have the cash flow. You are better to wait another 12 to 18 months and do it properly, because you also need to allow money for marketing. Marketing is a key component to your business success, and when you open your business you want to market it effectively. If you've been in business for yourself for a few years and it's not meeting your expectations, what's your monthly marketing budget and what's your attitude towards marketing? Do you look at marketing as an investment or an expense? This will be discussed in more detail in Part II of this book.

INCOME-PRODUCING VS NON-INCOME-PRODUCING EQUIPMENT

When it comes to purchasing equipment, there are two types of equipment purchases you can make. One is income-producing equipment and the other is non-income-producing equipment. For example, let's say you need to purchase eight waiting chairs – four for your reception and two chairs for each consult room – and you're deciding between a $150 chair and a $400 chair, which means you will spend $1200 or $3200. This is when you need to stop and think. Will the $150 chair be sufficient for your current needs? If yes, can you use the $2000 saving elsewhere in your business?

I know from experience that you are better off investing $2000 towards income-producing equipment, such as a Therapeutic Ultrasound, a Doppler or even a Therapeutic Wax Foot Bath. These inexpensive income-producing items will generate income from day one and will continue to do so for the life of the equipment, whereas a $400 chair will not.

SET EQUIPMENT GOALS

Before making any equipment purchases, ask the following question: *"How many patients do I need to treat and what will the fee need to be before I get my full investment back?"* I always know the answer to this question before I purchase any equipment, and then I set a goal for when this will be achieved. You should do the same, and you should make this a habit.

Purchasing equipment without setting goals is ludicrous. I recall a Podiatrist I knew who purchased a flash treadmill, three high-speed video cameras and Silicon Coach running software, and after 18 months it had not generated one additional dollar of income into his business because he had not thought about how he was going to implement this technology into his clinic and he had not considered his fees for this particular service. In the end he went broke.

In contrast, I purchased a $35,000 Arc Fox Laser for treating fungal nails and my goal was to recoup my full investment within three months. To reach my goal I had to see approximately 88 patients at an average fee of $400 per patient. I achieved this in the first three months, as planned, and then doubled my investment in six months, and my laser continues to bring in amazing profits week after week.

When I purchased my own CADCAM milling machine for making orthotics onsite, it cost $75,000. Taking materials into account and other running costs I calculated I needed to mill approximately 1000 pairs of orthotics to break even. I set a goal to do this in the first 12 months and once again it was achieved. In fact, it was achieved in just over 10 months, and we are now saving approximately $125,000 per year in lab fees.

If you think about it, income-producing equipment can and should be used to set your business apart from your competition, and the type of equipment you purchase says a lot about you and your business. In Cairns no other podiatry business has a laser for treating fungal nails, nor do they have their own milling machine onsite, so what does this say about my podiatry business?

What type of podiatry business do you want to have one day and how do you want to be perceived?

It's No Secret, There's Money In Podiatry, however...you must manage your finances.

---

*After reading this chapter, what ideas are going through your head? Write them down **right now**.*

_____

_____

_____

_____

_____

_____

_____

WHAT TYPE OF PODIATRY BUSINESS DO YOU WANT?

Opening your own podiatry business is a great decision, but have you given any thought to the *type* of business you want to have? Having a podiatry business with no clinical emphasis is a boring way to practice, and I should know because I let more than 10 years slide past before I took decisive action towards creating a podiatry business that matched my interests. I used to visit nursing homes because it was easy money and my business had bills to pay, but it was unfulfilling and at times depressing work. *It wasn't what I signed up for.*

I grew up playing a lot of sport, and it was through sport that an interest in podiatry developed. It was not an interest in clipping toenails...so why was I not more involved in the sports side of podiatry? When I was at university I developed a strong interest in biomechanics, and because I studied Art for five years at school I found I really enjoyed making and designing orthotics. Once again, why was I not involved more in biomechanics and orthotic manufacturing? *The answer is simple: I forgot. I became bogged down in the day-to-day crud of running a business and lost sight of my goals.*

As a result, in 1998 I considered leaving podiatry and doing something else. But then I remembered why I got into podiatry in the first place and what my interests were, so why leave? I just had to make a decision to chase the type of work I wanted and to stay focused on this, and that is exactly what I did. My podiatry business today is very profitable and has a comfortable 90:10 split between Biomechanical (BIO) and General (GEN) type patients.

GETTING YOUR PATIENT RATIO RIGHT

This patient ratio of BIO and GEN patients developed because this is the type of podiatry business I wanted to have. It did not occur by accident. I had to make the decision, and then I had to make it happen. Now *you* have to decide what type of podiatry business you want! Do you want a podiatry business that has a strong emphasis in sports and orthotics, or are you more interested in diabetes? You may have an interest in laser therapy for fungal nails, acupuncture or foot mobilisation. No area of podiatry is better than another, however you need to know what interests you because only then can you steer your clinic in that particular direction.

To have a financially successful podiatry business and to pull in a consistent six-figure income year after year, you need to focus your efforts into areas of podiatry you enjoy, areas that have a high profit margin, and areas with a high dollar value per hour – it's that simple. Don't get me wrong, you can make a good living clipping toenails and visiting nursing homes, but if you're not fulfilled with your daily routine and you want a pay rise, you need to change your BIO v GEN ratio. (And there's another benefit I failed to mention: you'll also work fewer hours per week.)

My first podiatry business on the Gold Coast had a BIO v GEN ratio of approximately 5:95, which reflected how I ran my business at the time. When I opened my business in Cairns I made far more money because I was busier, but my ratio of BIO and GEN patients did not change: it was still 5:95. However, after investing $695 to attend a weekend seminar on how to have a more profitable business my thinking changed and so did my business. Within three months of attending this weekend seminar, my business turnover doubled and I've never looked back.

You may find it hard to believe that one weekend seminar made such a difference to my life, but that's all it takes. Unfortunately, you do not know which weekend seminar it is going to be! There's a saying, "When the student is ready...the teacher will come", and this applies to everyone. I have spent a small fortune on self-education and development, and I will continue to do so because I understand the value. Hopefully you will see the value also.

When I established Proarch Podiatry Mackay in 2002 I took a gamble and decided that this particular podiatry clinic would provide no general foot care and instead would focus solely on sports, biomechanics and orthotics. I had no instruments on site, therefore the chance of doing any general work was zero. It was an anxious waiting game, but it worked and was a roaring financial success.

So, what type of podiatry business do you want? There is no right or wrong answer – you just need to decide, become focused and then commit to it 100%, as I did in Mackay.

AVOID TRADITIONALISTS

Traditionalists will tell you that your business should cover all aspects of podiatry and you're losing money by not seeing general foot care patients. They will also tell you that some general foot care patients do become orthotic patients over time. Well, both these statements are correct and you do lose money by not seeing general patients, and some general patients do become orthotics patients over time, however:

> "If you look through enough rubbish bins you
> will eventually find a good apple...but is that
> where you should be looking for good apples?"
>
> Zig Ziglar

Of course not: if you want good apples you go to the fruit shop. You go to the place where you know good apples are going to be located. Developing the type of podiatry business you want works on exactly the same principle. If you want a podiatry business with no general foot care patients then draw the line in the sand and commit to it. If you want both biomechanics and general patients, work out the ratio you would be happy to work with (such as 90:10, 80:20 or 50:50), and then tailor your marketing to achieve this patient outcome. If you're in business for yourself and you're not happy with your current BIO v GEN patient ratio, make a conscious decision to change it, because no one is going to do it for you, but remember it will take a little time to create the change.

> "They say that time changes things, but you
> actually have to change them yourself."
>
> Andy Warhol

ARE YOU GOING TO BE AN ORIGINAL OR AN IMITATION?

Initially it can be difficult to know the type of podiatry business you want, so if you can't answer this right now, don't stress about it. Sometimes you have to just go with the flow and see what eventuates – just don't wait 10 years like I did. Unfortunately many Podiatrists never get around to answering this question, which is why so many podiatry businesses are identical and constantly fight over the same patients.

Is your plan to open another boring podiatry business, an imitation of what you've previously seen, or is your podiatry business going to be more *original*? Ask yourself the following questions about your proposed podiatry business:

- How many Podiatrists in your area provide the same service?

- Are they all doing it the same way?

- Are they all using the same processes?

- What will distinguish your business from your competitors?

- What skills have you got that they don't?

- What equipment are you going to purchase?

If you cannot tell your business apart from your competitors, what chance do your patients have? Also, why would a Doctor, Physiotherapist, Chiropractor or Osteopath decide to refer their patients to you instead of the Podiatrist they've been using for the past few years if you're not offering something better? In Cairns there have been six new podiatry clinics open in the past five years and I can't tell them apart. They all advertise the same message. Does any of this sound familiar to you?

- General Foot Care

- Diabetic Foot Care

- Warts

- Ingrown Toenails

- Orthotics (soft and hard)

- Sports Problems.

These ads are BOOORRRRRIINNGG because they're all saying the same thing. If you want to have a successful podiatry business, you have to decide what type of podiatry business you want and you need to make an effort to stand out from the crowd.

> "You have to learn the rules of the game. And then, you have to play better than anyone else."
>
> Albert Einstein

CHOOSING A BUSINESS NAME

Your business name is an important part of the identity of your business, and it can help to set you apart and demonstrate the type of business you are. Everyone wants a cool business name, so it seems, but it's important to note that your business name is the first image that you put *"out there"* about your podiatry business, so it must be a reflection of the type of business you want to have one day. If you want to attract more sports, biomechanics and orthotics patients, I don't think using Pretty Feet Podiatry is going to cut the mustard. Remember your business name has the ability to attract or repel patients, so you do need to give it some serious thought, but don't try to be too clever.

> "Hanging a sign on a cow that says 'I am a horse' does not make it a horse."
>
> Unknown

When it comes to creating a business name you should make sure it is easy to remember and easy to read. A simple name is a good name. It should also be unique if possible, and definitely not too generic. Avoid using the words "clinic" or "centre" at the end of your business name because they are nothing words and can make your business name sound similar to others that use the same words. Always check if someone else is using a similar business name to the one you are considering. A simple online search will show this, and you'll be surprised how many podiatry businesses have similar names. More and more patients go online to look for podiatry services and search for information, so if they type in your business name, or something similar, will they get your business or will they get a podiatry business that sounds like yours?

Make sure you don't outgrow your business name. Is your business name too location specific, meaning it cannot be used in other areas? My original business name when I moved to Cairns was North Queensland Podiatry, but I realised this name would make no sense if I opened a clinic on the Sunshine Coast, so I changed it to Proarch Podiatry because it has no geographical boundaries.

The jury is still out on business names deliberately spelt incorrectly. It may look clever but if you're having to constantly spell it out for someone so they can find you online because of odd, incorrect spelling, is it really a clever name, especially if it could be spelt correctly and have the exact same meaning?

Once you have developed your business name, you need to protect it because your business name does have value. Just having it registered in your State gives you no protection nationally, so the best option is to register it as a Trademark. You can register a trademark over the Internet yourself quite easily – which I have done on numerous occasions – or you can seek legal help, but this will cost you more.

If you cannot decide on a good business name, simply use your own name, because you can always change it later.

It's No Secret, There's Money In Podiatry, however…you need to know the type of business you want and the type of patients you want to treat.

*After reading this chapter, what ideas are going through your head? Write them down **right now**.*

_____

_____

_____

_____

_____

_____

_____

_____

DISCOUNTS, PRICE WARS AND ACCOUNTS

DISCOUNTING

Personally I would never ask a health professional for a discount because I value their knowledge too much, and furthermore I wouldn't visit a health professional who used discounts as part of their marketing.

So, should you offer discounts? Discounting is a personal decision, and it really comes back to the type of podiatry business you want. If you're being asked for discounts on a regular basis then you need to adjust your marketing because you're obviously attracting the wrong type of patient. Some patients ask for a discount even before they know what your fees are!

The following groups of people will often request a discount:

- pensioners

- seniors

- healthcare card holders

- mature aged students

- disabled

- unemployed

- EPC (Medicare referred) patients

- And…I almost left out a group: "The Tight Arse". This group can afford your services but simply don't want to pay reasonable prices.

Remember, you already accept a lower fee when treating Veterans' Affairs and Work Cover patients, so if you're also going to give a discount to the patients above, how many patients are actually paying full price?

A Podiatrist once asked me to look at their fee structure because their patient numbers were up each month but their profits were unchanged, and they thought maybe they had to put their fees up. It only took five minutes to identify the problem. A fee increase wasn't required, they just needed to stop discounting because only 10% of their patients were paying full price. I calculated they were losing about $1500 per week as a result. They made the required changes, and turnover increased by $6000 the first month and $8000 the next! However, out of habit they started offering discounts again, and three months later were back in financial trouble.

The effect on your bottom line

Many Podiatrists don't see how discounting impacts their bottom line, which is why I strongly discourage it. As a generalised example, if a consultation was $60 and if you had a profit margin of 30%, your gross profit would be $18 from that consultation. If you gave a patient a small 10% discount of $6, so they only paid $54, this would be a 33% reduction to your gross profit, $18 minus $6, leaving you a profit of $12. If you gave them a

15% discount of $9, this would be a 50% reduction in your gross profit, $18 minus $9, leaving a profit of $9. The patient only sees the small 10% or 15% discount; what they don't see is your bottom line and that you actually lose a massive 33% to 50% by discounting. (And, in all honesty, they don't care.)

Therefore discounting is crazy. A 50% loss in gross profits is lunacy and equates to you having to do twice the amount of work to make the same profits as another Podiatrist that does not discount. Stick to your policy of "no discounts" because it will pay off for you long-term – you will work less and make more profits.

PRICE WARS

If you have a new podiatry business open in your area and they are discounting their fees to attract more new patients, don't try to compete by lowering your fees. Let them have their loss of profits and you concentrate on attracting patients who don't look for discounts. Getting into a price war to attract new patients is one of the dumbest marketing strategies I've seen, and long-term has to be detrimental to the morale of their team because they would constantly be working with patients who have that discount mentality and who just want the cheapest price. *Getting into a price war with an idiot results in two idiots.*

Have you considered how the new podiatry business became the cheapest? It's easy; they telephoned every podiatry business in the area, pretended to be a patient and asked their fees, then undercut everyone by a few dollars. If you have a podiatry business like this in your area, you should relish them because they will be filling their appointment book with the *"cream of the crap"*, leaving you with all the good patients.

I once had a past employee ring my clinic pretending to be a patient. After the telephone call I wrote him a letter saying, *"Following our telephone conversation today, here is a full copy of my fee schedule for your records".* My fee schedule is no secret, so if you want a copy just ask.

SHOULD YOU GIVE PATIENT ACCOUNTS?

I have the same account policy as the local supermarket: no accounts. You should adopt the same approach. Since having a "no account policy", my podiatry business has...wait for it...*no accounts*, and more importantly, my Receptionists are not wasting time chasing outstanding accounts. We do offer a payment plan for some patients that cannot afford the upfront cost of orthotics, however there are very strict qualifying criteria, and the patient must have a valid credit card and authorise us to deduct regular fortnightly payments. We've been using this payment method for the past ten-plus years and we've had no bad debts. If you want to protect your future, you need to value your services and charge accordingly.

If you feel you need to discount, be involved in price wars and offer accounts just to attract new patients and to keep your existing patients coming back, you have a business that is very sick and is in need of a big shot of penicillin. Believe me, you don't have to do it. I've been in business for 25 years and I've never done it, and I have a very profitable, very busy podiatry business, so there is no reason why you cannot do the same.

> **"Whether you think you can, or think you can't...you're right."**
>
> Henry Ford

It's No Secret, There's Money in Podiatry, but you've got to avoid discounting.

*After reading this chapter, what ideas are going through your head? Write them down **right now**.*

_____

_____

_____

_____

_____

_____

_____

_____

5 ATTRACTING THE RIGHT PATIENTS

THE BLOWFLY PRINCIPLE AND BAD PATIENTS

It's great having a brother in the health industry because it allows us to talk on a similar level about dealing with difficult patients. Even though we're at opposite ends of the body we face similar patient issues. We both agree that learning how to deal with difficult patients is important, but it's not as important as learning how to identify them as early as possible in the treatment process.

You learn quickly that all difficult patients – actually let's call them what they are, "bad patients" – exhibit the same traits. See if any of the following sound familiar to you:

- they complain about your fees

- they are rude

- they are always requesting discounts

- they ask for an account

- they pay accounts late (if you give accounts)

- they turn up late for their appointments without an explanation; however, they complain if you're running five minutes late

- they cancel their appointment at the last minute without a valid reason, and tell you it's none of your business if you ask why they're cancelling – *again!*

- they often "no show" for their appointments, once again with no valid reason

- they never apologise

- after no showing or cancelling late, they complain if they cannot make another appointment for the following day, even after you've explained how busy you are

- making an appointment for them is always difficult because it doesn't fit in with their busy work or gym schedule

- they complain and raise their voice at the most inopportune time – when the reception waiting area is full – because they love an audience.

You know the patients I'm talking about. We've all had them and we will continue to have them, however your goal is to limit your exposure to them. You need to identify them early and get rid of them as soon as possible. If you can, you should redirect them to your competition, because if your competition is busy seeing all the Bad Patients, the ones you reject, just like John West, this frees up your time to see more Good Patients.

My brother and I refer to Bad Patients and Blowflies, and together we have come up with a law called *The Blowfly Principle.* This may sound a little crude, but it fits. You're standing in your front yard talking to your neighbour and you notice dog poop on your footpath. Nothing unusual there. Suddenly a blowfly passes in front of you and lands on the dog sh#t. Of course you keep talking and think nothing of it, but then all of a sudden something else flies past your face! What do you think it was?

Was it a bird? No!

Was it a plane? No!

Was it another blowfly? Yes, because blowflies attract more blowflies!

Bad Patients are similar to blowflies, because Bad Patients will attract more Bad Patients, because people associate socially with people that are similar to them. They'll talk about the weather, which movies they've seen and which services they like and dislike. Bad Patients, if you keep them, will tell all their friends that you are the best podiatry business in the world because:

- they can arrive late and you never complain about it, which is perfect if the midday movie runs over the scheduled time

- they can cancel on the day without any penalty, which is important if the girls at the local club decide to meet for coffee at the last minute

- if they decide not to attend at all because something better came up there is no penalty, which is perfect for those days when you just couldn't be bothered picking up the telephone and letting the clinic know you're not coming

- if you complain about their fees they will give you a 10% discount, which is great because booze and cigarettes are getting expensive.

Do you really need to have these types of patients in your podiatry business, or would you prefer they visited your opposition? I have politely removed many patients from my business and I make no apologies for this, because it's my business and therefore everyone must play by my rules. You will find that Bad Patients, or blow-flies, are a very small percentage of your total patients and the majority will be a pleasure to work with, however it comes back to the type of podiatry business you want to have and how strict you are with discounts and accounts. Remember...blowflies love a good discount.

> "There are more honest people and more good people than there are thieves and bad people. It's just always been that way."
>
> Michael Nesmith

SO WHO IS YOUR TARGET MARKET?

If I asked you to picture your perfect patient, who would that be? Do you have an image in your head, or is it a little fuzzy? Think about the following questions:

- What would they look like?
- What age group would they be in?
- Is there a specific gender?
- Would they play sport?
- If yes, what type of sports?
- Are they members of a gym?
- What's their income?
- Are they blue collar or white collar?

- What do they do socially?

- Are they members of any specific community groups?

- Where do they live geographically?

The more questions you ask the more answers you get, and the more answers you get the better image you'll create of the perfect patient. This mythical creature, the perfect patient, does exist and they're waiting for you to find them.

Your perfect patient is what's referred to as your *target market*.

Multiple target markets

If your image is still a little fuzzy it may be because you have more than one perfect patient. You may have multiple perfect patients, you just didn't realise. So, if there's a possibility that you may have two or three perfect patients then this also means you may have two or three target markets. Imagine a clinic, bursting at the seams with perfect patients, day after day – *how awesome would that be?* Not only would it be awesome, it would be fun to go to work and your pockets would be overflowing with cash.

I've heard Podiatrists say their target market is broad, which basically means they have no target market. Well, actually that's not true – they do have a target market, and I call them *The Breathing*. Targeting The Breathing may sound like a smart move because you're covering all your bases, but it's very general and an ineffective way to try to market your podiatry business. Not having a defined target market is like playing darts without a dartboard. You go through the motions and expend the same amount of energy, but in the end there is no result – it's a pointless activity.

Having a specific target market or multiple markets doesn't mean you will never treat patients that do not fit your target market, it just means you're focusing your marketing dollars and personal energy towards specific areas within your business that have great profit margins and a higher dollar per hour yield. When I first understood this concept of target marketing – or multiple target marketing – my business turnover went through the roof.

This is not rocket science. If you see a biomechanical patient and fit an orthotic you will be paid around $700 plus, depending on your fee schedule of course, and you will spend approximately one hour with the patient. So using this as an example, you will be making approximately $700 per hour. In contrast, how many toenails do you need to clip to make $700, and how much time will it take?

I know some podiatrists will look at these figures and say it's not possible to make $700 per hour, every hour, for eight hours a day, and they would be right. Sometimes it's only $250 per hour, while at times it's $1800 per hour. The point is: your income per hour is based on the services you offer.

What services can you offer, or target, that produce great profits and have a high dollar yield per hour? This is what you need to consider if you really want to boost the profitability of your business.

"In marketing I've seen only one strategy that can't miss and that is to market to your best customers first and the rest of the world last."

John Romero

PATIENTS TYPES A, B, C AND D

Understanding your target market or markets is important because if you don't know who you want to attract you'll waste money marketing to the wrong groups of people, but it's also important to understand that not everyone in your target market is going to be an ideal patient. Just because a patient fits into your target market doesn't mean they are going to be a patient you want to keep. Within every target market there are also going to be distinct patient types. For simplicity, I've divided them into A, B, C and D type patients. The longer you're in practice, the easier it becomes to identify them.

Let's have a look.

A Patients are your awesome patients. These patients make you want to get out of bed in the morning and be at work early. They always arrive on time, never complain about your fees, pay immediately, and they actually say *"thank you"* after their consultation, even after they have paid you. Their only drawback is their eagerness to refer patients to you, which sounds great, but unless you educate them, they may send the wrong type of patient.

B Patients are good patients, but not quite as awesome as A Patients. They do everything A Patients do, just not at the same high level, yet they are still a pleasure to work with.

C Patients are a pain in the butt. They arrive late without explanation, never apologise, they try to reschedule with little notice, they rarely follow your instructions and advice, and they complain about your fees always going up, even when they have not changed in two years.

D Patients are rude, ignorant and are slightly more irritating than your C Patients. C and D Patients are basically Bad Patients (blowflies) and should be redirected away from your business as soon as possible before they start referring more patients like themselves.

You should always try to work with your patients and at least attempt to upgrade them to the next level if you can. You should try to teach your C patients what they need to do to become a B patient, so they can continue to be a patient at your podiatry business, but if they are unwilling to make the required changes… refer them elsewhere. If you want to make good money and have a successful podiatry business you need to remove C and D type patients from your business.

Why you want more A and B patients and fewer C and D patients

Let's have a look at the many reasons why you need more A and B patients in your business:

- You will get far more good referrals from A and B patients who gladly pay your fees, whereas C and D patients who think you overcharge will only refer blowflies.

- A and B patients believe in what you do and they don't second-guess your motives. C and D will question everything.

- A and B patients respect you and your profession. C and D patients ask questions like, *"Did you have to go to university to be a Podiatrist?"*

- A and B patients expect good quality and are willing to pay for it. C and D patients want to be offered cheaper alternatives.

- When you put your fees up you do not need to explain yourself to A and B clients because they see value in the service you provide, whereas C and D patients will say, *"What, you're putting your fees up again?"*, even though it may have been two years since the previous fee increase.

- A and B patients make work fun because you get to utilise the full range of skills you have learnt. C and D patients will ask, *"Do I have to pay extra for that service?"*

- A and B patients return for review visits when recalled, whereas C and D patients only return when there is a problem or if there is a "special offer" on the table.

- A and B patients understand there is always a fee involved for an additional service, whereas C and D patients will lie and say you told them it was included in the initial costs and there would be no additional charge.

- You build lifelong relationships with A and B patients, their family and friends, which will give your business longevity, whereas you never get to know anything about C and D patients other then their ailments.

- A and B patients offer you constructive advice on how you could offer more services and make more money, whereas C and D patients will ask for discounts and offer you advice on how you could get more C and D patients by dropping your *ridiculous high fees*.

- A and B patients allow you to make more money by working fewer hours, whereas C and D patients want you to make less money but work more hours.

- A and B patients love hearing about conferences you've attended, whereas C and D patients are not interested in your continued education.

Do you really need any further convincing? If you can fill your day with A and B patients there won't be room for C and D patients. And even if a few C and D patients manage to slip through your guard they will not stay very long because they will not like the positive vibe of your podiatry business – C and D patients love misery, and misery loves company, and that's not happening in your happy podiatry business.

"When people show you who they are, believe them."

Bianca Frazier

It's No Secret, There's Money In Podiatry, however...you must surround yourself with the types of patients you want.

> *After reading this chapter, what ideas are going through your head? Write them down **right now**.*
>
> _____
>
> _____
>
> _____
>
> _____
>
> _____
>
> _____
>
> _____

THE VITAL FEW AND TRIVIAL MANY

I first read about *the vital few and trivial many* in a magazine about 20 years ago on a flight from Cairns to Sydney. I was on my way to attend our National Podiatry Conference, and after reading the article I put the magazine down and gave it no further thought. However, on the first evening of the conference, after a full day of lectures, I watched the "Podiatry Gods" (*Guest Speakers*) enter the post-conference venue – otherwise known as the bar – and I couldn't believe how quickly they were surrounded by other Podiatrists eager to get a few minutes of their time, and how free drinks were thrust into their hands without them even asking. Then it hit me: I'd just witnessed the *vital few and trivial many* first hand. I couldn't wait to get back on that plane and read the article a second time, and when I did, it made sense.

In 1906 Italian Economist Vilfredo Pareto created a mathematical formula that described the unequal wealth in his country. He observed that 80% of the wealth was owned by 20% of the population. At the time this was called the *Pareto Principle*. Then, in the 1930s, Dr Joseph Juran observed that 20% of all inputs, or activities, was always responsible for 80% of all outputs, or results. He called this principle the *"Vital Few and the Trivial Many"*. Both principles have since been used widely in business, management, engineering and science, and from these came the more commonly used term today: the 80:20 rule.

The 80:20 rule basically means:

■ 80% of your headaches will come from 20% of your patients – *most likely your C and D Patients*

■ 80% of your business errors will come from 20% of your team – *which is why you need to constantly re-train*

■ 80% of your patient referrals will come from 20% of your referral sources – *you need to nurture these relationships*

■ 80% of your income comes from 20% of the services you offer – *most likely your services with a high profit margin and high dollar yield per hour*

■ 80% of your marketing will produce 20% of your results; however, 20% of your marketing will produce 80% of your results. (A process called *Testing and Measuring* will be discussed in a later chapter to help you figure out what is working and what isn't).

This rule is by no means an exact science but it can be quite an accurate guide. But does it apply to the podiatry profession? *I'll let you be the judge of that, but I think it does.*

Who are the vital few in podiatry? They are the 20% of podiatry professionals who:

■ earn significantly more money – healthy six figure incomes

■ have podiatry businesses that look very professional

- have podiatry businesses with modern and up-to-date equipment

- contribute to the profession and make things happen in both the private and public sectors

- are involved in research projects that will make a difference

- are regularly invited to speak at state, national and international conferences

- everyone knows their name

- everyone wants to be on their LinkedIn list

- everyone wants to be friends with them on Facebook and *Likes* their business Facebook page

- everyone has them in their circles on Google+

- they're followed on Twitter because people want to know their opinion and thoughts

- people follow their blog posts

- their websites are alive, vibrant and constantly evolving

- they are always remembered after people have met them

- and…they will be sadly missed we they retire from the profession leaving a significant gap to fill.

Who are the trivial many? They are the 80% of Podiatrists that:

- earn the least amount of money *and they constantly complain about it*

- have podiatry businesses that look unprofessional

- have podiatry businesses with outdated equipment

- contribute nothing to the profession, but will be responsible for 80% of the complaints to the podiatry registration board

- carry on research projects that have little significance or benefits

- are never invited to speak at conferences, not even local events

- no one knows their name, and when introduced they are easily forgotten

- Facebook, Google+, Twitter, Blogs and other social media are rarely used or updated, because no one cares about their posts

- their websites, if they have one, are under construction or last updated in 2010

- will not be missed when they retire; in fact no one will notice they have left the profession because they will leave no gap.

Which group of podiatrists do you want to belong to? Not everyone can be a "Podiatry God" who is invited to speak at national and international podiatry conferences, however you can still be one of the vital few who earns significantly more money than the average Podiatrist. To do this you need to constantly remind yourself to stay focused on the 20% of your business activities that really matter and not get bogged down in the 80% that don't.

I'm aware 20% of the Podiatrists reading this book will enjoy it and apply what they've read and 80% will not, which only strengthens my belief in the 80:20 rule. Building a successful podiatry business doesn't occur by accident, it begins by understanding and living by some simple proven principles, such as the 80:20 rule.

GETTING YOUR TEAM INVOLVED

As the business owner you may understand the importance of the 80:20 rule and how it can transform your business and make it more productive by focusing your time and energy on daily activities, the 20% that matter and avoiding the 80% that don't, however you need to also get your team involved as well.

Team members often get *activity* and *productivity* mixed up. Scanning patient files, typing reports, wiping down benches, checking the mail and emptying bins are all activities that do need to be done, however picking up the telephone and calling a patient due for an orthotic review appointment is far more important and it needs to be prioritised this way.

For this reason you need to offer guidance and leadership, and you should discuss the 80:20 rule over and over again at clinic meetings. Discuss what activities belong in the 20% and what should be moved into the 80%. Make sure you get input from all team members and listen to what they have to say, then as a group formalise these two lists and make it a priority to constantly review them. Your 20% list should be far shorter than the 80% list; if not, you need to go back and look at your priorities.

It's No Secret, There's Money In Podiatry, however...you need to know where the money comes from.

*After reading this chapter, what ideas are going through your head? Write them down **right now**.*

_____

_____

_____

_____

_____

_____

_____

_____

SELECTING THE RIGHT TEAM MEMBERS

More than likely your first team member is going to be your Receptionist. If you don't think you can afford a Receptionist then maybe you should rethink being in business. I'll discuss this in more detail later, but you cannot afford to be sitting in your clinic waiting for patients to come to you…you've got to be seen, you've got to hit the pavements and drum up business.

When I had my Gold Coast business I didn't know what I was doing, however I did manage to do two things right. Firstly, I had a casual Receptionist, and secondly, I got out of my business and saw every Doctor, Physiotherapist and Chiropractor within a 15-kilometre radius. It took three months, but it was a worthwhile activity.

FINDING A RECEPTIONIST

Your front office position is crucial and should not be taken lightly. A Receptionist is more than just someone who answers the telephone and makes appointments. They represent you and your business, and they are the first person your patients see when they enter your business. Even with the best advice, guidance and screening processes, you can never guarantee the person you employ is going to be right for you and your business. I have employed Receptionists using ads in the local newspaper, by word of mouth, and I have used the services of a professional employment agency. Regardless of the method, some Receptionists have been great and others poor.

When you're hiring someone as your Receptionist you should immediately pay attention to appearance. They must look professional and dress appropriately. Their hair should be tidy and their nails should be clean, because what you see at this first interview is as good as it's going to get – it will never improve from that first meeting. Look at their footwear and pay special attention to how they smell. Are they a smoker? Being an ex-smoker myself, I recall how the addiction draws you away from your work; an addicted smoker will constantly have the urge to sneak out for a quick hit, which is unproductive. The more stressed the situation, the more often they will require a cigarette.

Your Receptionist needs a warm and welcoming personality, and they should be very comfortable using the telephone. Up-to-date computer skills and good grammar are very important, because they will be proofreading your reports and at times you will need them to write something on your behalf.

At interviews I like to ask two simple questions: "Tell me what you know about podiatry," and, "What did you think of our website?" The first question seems obvious, but you'll be surprised how often they will tell you they know nothing about podiatry, which surprises me because who seriously applies for a position in a field they know nothing about, or without having done at least a little homework about the profession?

The second question, in my opinion, is more important than the first, because it shows initiative and a little forward thinking.

It's rare for a successful business not to have a website, so it makes sense to at least look at your future employer's website to get an idea of what it is they do. If I was applying for a position I cared about, I would do my homework and also look at their website in some detail; however, if it was just a job to me and I didn't care, I would do neither.

Once you have identified the right person for the position, make them aware that there is a probationary period and make sure you do regular reviews of their work. If it's not working out, replace them; don't keep hoping things will improve because they rarely do. I have hung onto Receptionists *and* Podiatrists way longer than I should have and it always ends poorly.

An employee's success or failure though can often come down to your training methods, or lack of training methods, so make sure you have good training manuals and make sure all procedures and protocols are documented and are easy to follow.

EMPLOYING PODIATRISTS

When it comes to employing Podiatrists, the same rules apply with appearance and dress sense, however in additional to all of the above they must also be able to communicate with their patients, because lack of communication results in poor treatment outcomes. Also, look at their work history as a student. Did they work behind a bar, did they clean cinemas after hours, or did they work at a sports store selling footwear? Podiatrists with previous employment in footwear sales have always been my best podiatry team members. Podiatrists who worked behind bars had great communication skills, however those that avoided human contact by cleaning cinemas after hours have lacked personality, had poor communication skills with their patients and failed to impress.

All Podiatrists you employ must be prepared to follow your *treatment protocols*, and these protocols – which define *how you like to approach and treat particular foot and lower limb problems* – should be written down in some form of manual for easy reference. A new Podiatrist cannot simply start treating patients as they see fit, especially if it is in direct conflict with how you like to treat patients. As an employer you should make it a habit to regularly review the patient files of every new Podiatrist and closely look at treatment protocols and outcomes. If it looks correct, you can ease back a little, but never stop.

Reviewing treatment protocols and outcomes is especially important following a podiatry conference. Podiatrists tend to get excited when they see something new and will rarely look at the costs associated. Rock Tape is a perfect example of a great product with many beneficial uses, yet it is expensive, so its usage must be controlled and charged accordingly.

Following treatment protocols also makes it much easier for one Podiatrist to take over from another Podiatrist if they are on holidays, off sick or if they leave your employment. It's a sad fact but Podiatrists come and go, but as the business owner you will always be present, and if you need to step in and take control of a situation it is much easier if everyone is on the same page and reading from the same playbook.

It's No Secret, There's Money In Podiatry, however…you need a strong, effective team that works together.

*After reading this chapter, what ideas are going through your head? Write them down **right now**.*

_____

_____

_____

_____

_____

_____

_____

_____

8
NUMBERS DON'T LIE
(KPIs)

When I owned my podiatry business on the Gold Coast I had no understanding about the relationship between business profits and business performance. I came to realise that even a poorly run podiatry business can still make a profit, however it could make far more profits if the business owners had key performance indicators (KPIs) in place to measure performance, because numbers don't lie, only people lie. KPIs can be used to identify people and processes within a business that are underperforming. They can also be used to measure progress towards business goals by looking at critical numbers on a daily, weekly and monthly basis.

If you've never considered using KPIs it may take a while for you to really appreciate their value, however once you see how they can transform an average business into an awesome business, you'll be convinced. An interesting thing happens when you start measuring KPIs; both your personal and business performance improves. This improvement occurs as a direct result of knowing your numbers, because *you can only improve upon something once you have a number to improve upon*. For example, if last month

60% of your biomechanical patients got orthotics, you use this number to push yourself beyond 60% next month.

WHAT SHOULD YOU MEASURE?

So, where do you start and what should you measure? I personally don't think you can have too many KPIs, because the more information you have about your business the more educated your business decisions. To get you started I've listed the KPIs that I think are a priority, and also a little insight as to why these particular KPIs are important to use in your business immediately.

Number of new patients: How many new patients you see is an important KPI and it needs to be looked at on a weekly basis. However, simply calculating the total number of new patients is not enough, you need to categorise the types of new patients. For example, how many new patients are biomechanical patients (BIO) and how many are general patients (GEN)? If you use laser therapy for fungal nails, you also need a third category for new laser patients.

When you start looking at KPIs more closely you should see a direct correlation between your marketing campaigns aimed at your target markets and your new patient numbers in each category. *I know when I run our heel pain marketing campaign we have an increase in BIO patients with heel pain, and the same results occur when I use our marketing campaign for laser therapy to treat fungal nails.* I never advertise for GEN patients because they're not my target market, so rarely will I see a sudden increase in general patients.

Number of new patients that reappointed for additional services: Every business needs a steady flow of new patients, however what's equally important is what you do with these new patients once they come into your podiatry business. It costs far more money to attract new patients to your business than it does to keep your existing patients coming back, therefore you need to place emphasis on re-booking patients and have systems in place for recalling patients if they have not attended for a certain period of time. A one-off consultation with no further visits or additional services is a wasted opportunity.

Every new general patient should be aware of the importance of ongoing foot care; therefore you need to know the following KPIs:

- How many re-booked for ongoing general foot care?

- How many general patients re-booked for a biomechanical assessment? *(Honestly, is there a more opportune time to explain the full services your podiatry business offers than when a patient is sitting directly in front of you for 15 or 30 minutes?)*

- How many re-booked for a Doppler assessment or paraffin wax foot bath?

Every biomechanical patient should be looked at the same way:

- How many re-booked for a biomechanical review (*if necessary*)?

- How many are re-booked for general foot care?

- How many obtain orthotics? *More importantly, how many don't?*

- How many had additional treatment services, such as ultrasound, shockwave therapy, acupuncture and foot mobilisation?

Number of patients that purchase retail products: Every podiatry business should have retail products that can be sold to their patients. When I first introduced retail products I made approximately $500 profit for the year, however $500 led to $1200, which led to $3500, which led to $10,000, and it kept growing. We eventually introduced footwear, so of course our retail sales are now in the hundreds of thousands of dollars each year, which contributes significantly to our podiatry business.

You need to introduce retail products if you haven't already done so, and you need to calculate how many of your patients purchase your retails products. Also, what products are being purchased? As I mentioned previously, when you start measuring your KPIs they immediately improve, and retail sales are no different.

Orthotic conversion rates: This particular KPI trumps all others. If you decide you're only going to have one KPI, make it this one. Your *orthotic conversion rate* is a simple calculation based on how many patients get orthotics after having a biomechanical assessment. You should really have two orthotic conversion rates, one for new biomechanical patients and one for existing patients who have a biomechanical assessment. The conversion rate for existing patients should always be higher than for new patients because you have already built a relationship with the patient.

When it comes to conversion rates, you need to have acceptable benchmarks in place and every Podiatrist needs to hit these benchmarks. If your numbers show that a Podiatrist consistently underperforms you need to determine if it's their ability or if it's their beliefs that are the problem, because you can always improve someone's ability but it is very hard to change someone's beliefs. Underperformers need to be let go as soon as possible.

If you're planning on having multiple Podiatry businesses one day, you really need to understand the power of conversion rates and you need to have an extensive list of KPIs in place. I was once asked if you can have too many KPIs and the answer is no. You should have KPIs on every aspect of your business, then once you know the numbers you can then determine if they are important to continue with or not. I have over 20 different KPIs I measure in my podiatry business. Some are evaluated on a weekly basis while others are looked at monthly. I also have some KPIs that are only introduced sporadically, when I'm introducing something new or making a change with a system or process.

KPIs CAN HELP IDENTIFY UNDERPERFORMERS

Once you start looking at your weekly KPIs, underperforming team members will be found out very quickly, which is why it's important for all team members to be aware that you have KPIs in place. Don't keep it a secret; it needs to be common knowledge and the results need to be published somewhere, such as the lunchroom noticeboard, so they can be viewed by everyone. It's amazing how performance improves when everyone is held accountable.

KPIs CAN HELP IDENTIFY INCOMPATIBLE STAFF

Underperforming team members cost your podiatry business a lot of money, and the problem may not simply be lack of ability. You may have team members who do not agree with your business philosophy and thinking. They may not agree with the way you run your business, or how your fees are structured. Honestly, they may think you're an idiot, but you pay their wage so they put up with it.

Many years ago I had a Podiatrist employed, and unbeknown to me he didn't believe in custom orthotics and instead preferred pre-made orthotics. At the time my business was busy and I was only focusing on the monthly profits, I wasn't looking at overall business performance. However, after attending a weekend workshop I began paying a little more attention to my business. Only then did I notice the high number of premade orthotics being prescribed, so I telephone the most recent 15 patients fitted to ask why they chose premade orthotics over a custom orthotic. Surprisingly, all 15 patients told me they were never given an option. I therefore offered all 15 patients an opportunity to return for a free re-assessment, which they did, and 14 out of 15 decided to have custom orthotics made and were prepared to pay the higher price. When I spoke with the Podiatrist and asked why he didn't offer custom orthotics, he told me he thought custom orthotics were a rip off. That made no sense, and our working relationship ended that same day.

If KPIs had been in place and measured weekly, I would have identified his problem within a matter of weeks and saved my business a lot of money. I estimate he lost me approximately $40,000 in revenue over a nine-month period, but it could have been much worse. *This is why knowing the numbers is important.*

WHAT'S THE DIFFERENCE BETWEEN STATISTICS AND KPIs?

Basically, statistics look at the past – *where you've been* – whereas KPIs look at the present – *where you are right now. KPIs are looking at today, this week and this month.* Because KPIs show current, up-to-date information, you can use these numbers to verify if your business is on track to achieve a particular weekly or monthly target. KPIs also give you the ability to make sudden changes within your business that will have a direct influence on tomorrow and therefore this week's figures. Statistics, on the other hand, have no influence on the future as they only show what has already happened – what you've already achieved or not achieved. Statistics only give you an idea of what may occur in the future; they cannot be used to instigate change.

For example, you may have a goal to see 80 new patients this month. You've implemented certain strategies and have a great marketing campaign in place, which you're closely monitoring. Obviously you feel this goal is achievable, because statistics show that for the same period last year you saw 70 new patients, so 80 new patients is a stretch but it's well within reach, however knowing this past statistical figure will have no influence on achieving this month's target of 80 new patients.

As the weeks progress, your weekly KPIs will keep you informed as to whether you will or will not achieve your target of 80 new patients for the month. If your weekly KPIs show you're falling short of your goal, you can start making changes immediately. These changes can be monitored and further changes made if required. This is the power of having KPIs in place.

> "Most people use statistics the way a drunkard uses
> a lamppost, more for support than illumination."
>
> Mark Twain

It's No Secret, There's Money in Podiatry, however...you need to know your daily, weekly and monthly numbers.

*After reading this chapter, what ideas are going through your head? Write them down **right now**.*

_____

_____

_____

_____

_____

_____

_____

_____

THE THREE WAYS TO INCREASE TURNOVER AND PROFITS

Everything you've read so far is important and necessary if you want to own a successful podiatry business, but in it's most simplistic form increasing your business turnover and having greater profits involves three basic areas of improvement:

1. **Attracting more new patients:**

   a. Better marketing

   b. Smarter marketing

   c. More effective marketing

2. **Get your new patients to spend more money each time they visit your business:**

   a. Offering further retail options

   b. Increasing the types of services you offer

   c. Internal marketing

   d. Increasing your fees

3. **Get your new and existing patients to return to your business more often:**

   a. Recommend further appointments

   b. Follow up missed appointments

   c. Have a good recall and reactivation system in place

   d. Increase your patient contact

No matter how you look at it, it's that simple.

Let's look at an example to demonstrate how a small change in each of these three areas of your business can produce outstanding results. Let's assume the next 10 new patients at your podiatry business spend $100 per consultation. This would equate to $1000 in gross fees. If all 10 patients visit your podiatry business three times over the next 12 months then your annual turnover would be $3000 from these patients.

Now, if you worked a little smarter on all three areas of your business and you managed to increase each area by only 10%, this would equate to 11 new patients instead of 10, and they would spend $110 per consultation instead of $100, and they would return to your practice 3.3 times per year instead of only three times.

Let's look at the numbers: 11 new patients × $110 × 3.3 visits per patient = $3993, which is a $993 increase in turnover, or 33%, which is good. If you use the same formula but increase all three areas by 20%, it gets even more exciting: 12 new patients × $120 × 3.6 visits per patient = $5184, which is a $2184 increase in turnover, or 72.8%, which is great.

As you can see, a small change in all three areas of your business produces outstanding results because of the compounding effect. A common mistake with Podiatrists is their lack of attention on all three areas of their business. Yes, you do need to attract new patients to your business, but if this is your only area of focus you're going to have to work so much harder to produce the same results.

Once again, *numbers don't lie*: to achieve a $2184 improvement by just increasing new patient numbers and neglecting the other two areas, you would have to attract 17 new patients instead of 10, which equates to a massive 70% increase. Trying to increase your new patients by 70% each and every month is hard work; believe me, this is how I used to run my podiatry business. All my focus and attention was on new patients, but once I realised I could work smarter by working on small incremental increases in all three areas of my business, I produced better results with much less work on a more consistent basis.

INCREASING YOUR FEES

Many podiatrists put off increasing their consultation fees because they're concerned patients will get angry and go somewhere else. Here's the truth of the matter: if you're not getting 10% of your patients complaining about your fees then you're too cheap, and only C and D patients will eventually leave because receiving a quality service is not important to them, only price is. However, your A and B patients will stay if they feel your fees are justified.

A few years ago a friend of mine purchased a podiatry business from a retiring Podiatrist. It was a very profitable business, even though the fees were quite low. This business also had a very large percentage of general patients, so the new owner decided to put the fees up by 20% on all consultations and services, thinking this would make many of the general patients go elsewhere, and in return the increased fees would balance the loss of patients; however, it backfired and the business got busier.

What the new owner failed to realise was that when they increased their fees many patients perceived that they must have been more experienced, and so they paid the new fees, and they also referred their friends and family. A percentage of the general patients also became orthotic patients, and yes some patients did leave, but the bottom line was a $100,000 per year increase in gross fees, which makes me wonder how much money the previous owner let slip through their fingers, leading up to retirement.

Don't make the same mistake yourself. Don't simply charge the same fee as everyone else if you feel you offer more and provide a better service. If you have a satellite business that involves travelling, your fees shouldn't be the same as your main business, because fuel and travel time should be taken into account.

It's No Secret, There's Money In Podiatry, however...you must understand the concept of compounding.

---

*After reading this chapter, what ideas are going through your head? Write them down **right now**.*

_____

_____

_____

_____

_____

_____

_____

10

THE ORTHOTIC ECONOMY

Before moving into systems and marketing, I thought I would touch on a concept I've been using for years. It drives my wife nuts at times, but it serves me very well – I call it *The Orthotic Economy*, and this is how it works.

There's an interstate conference or business training seminar and you're deciding if you should go or not because of the costs to attend. Let's say it will cost you $3000, by the time you pay for the conference, accommodation, airfares and food. Now you're thinking, *this is ridiculous, $3000 to attend a conference, there's no way I'm paying that.* However, here's how The Orthotic Economy works. How many orthotics would you need to fit to pay for the conference? If your fee for a pair of orthotics is $500, you only need to fit an extra six pairs of orthotics to pay for the whole conference (6 × $500 = $3000), which is easy to achieve.

This may seem like a strange economic formula, but it does put things into perspective, and it works. It's only six pairs of orthotics, and if you go to the conference with that mindset you'll be amazed what you can achieve when you return. You may learn something that makes you fit an extra six pairs of orthotics per month, making you an additional $36,000 per year. If this was the case the initial $3000 would be insignificant.

Have you ever considered having a one-on-one business coach? It may cost you $500, a $1000, or maybe even $1500 per month based on the service they provide, and I've heard Podiatrists say that those sorts of figures are utterly ridiculous. However, it's only one, two or three pairs of orthotics per month if you use The Orthotic Economy. I first used a business coach myself 15 years ago and their fee at that time was $1000 per month, which was two orthotics, so I thought if I can fit an extra two orthotics per month using their advice then it's not costing me anything. The end result was I fitted an extra 30 pairs per month and made an additional $15,000 per month. Once again The Orthotic Economy served me well.

Over the years I have had numerous business coaches, and even though I'm writing this book I still regularly attend business seminars, the only difference is they're at a much higher level than they used to be. My current Business Coach, Rem Jackson, lives in the United States and we regularly communicate via email, teleconferences and FaceTime, and I also keep in regular contact with my writing coach Andrew Griffiths, who is Australia's #1 business and entrepreneurial author with 11 books published in 50 countries, so when it comes to writing he knows his stuff. If you don't invest in yourself, no one else will.

I use The Orthotic Economy in all areas of my life, not just at work. I recently bought a Gorilla costume – as you do – and it was $389, and I thought immediately, *that's less than one orthotic*, so I purchased it. When I go out for dinner and I look at the final bill, I don't see $250, I see half an orthotic.

This doesn't mean that I recommend splashing money around like there's no tomorrow, what I'm suggesting is that you should use The Orthotic Economy as a benchmark to help you make intelligent, informed business decisions. Once you've mastered it at work, start applying The Orthotic Economy to all areas of your life.

*After reading this chapter, what ideas are going through your head? Write them down **right now**.*

_____

_____

_____

_____

_____

_____

_____

11

SYSTEMS

Businesses that fail to have systems also fail to reach their full potential, because you cannot run a successful business by hoping everyone is doing a particular task correctly. Some businesses have "informal" systems, but a system not documented is also a system for failure. If you do not develop written systems, a set of guidelines for your team to follow, your team will just start making them up as they go and this causes confusion between team members and ultimately poor results.

SEVEN REASONS WHY YOU SHOULD DEVELOP SYSTEMS

1. **Improved productivity:** Everyone involved in the business will have a set of processes to follow which will deliver a predictable result each and every time it is followed correctly, which will improve productivity.

2. **Greater patient satisfaction and confidence:** This results in higher profits and return business. You will receive more referrals from patients who are satisfied with your service and have confidence in your advice.

3. **Fewer mistakes and errors:** With systems in place there is greater control over how information is distributed throughout the business, which results in less double-handling and reduces errors.

4. **Better accountability for team members:** If an error does occur, well-documented systems will allow you to identify the point at which the error occurred and who may be responsible for the error.

5. **Less reliance on the business owner:** Systems give the business owner freedom. A good system should document the question, the answer and the expected outcome, so team members can make decisions without the business owner being present.

6. **Improved training:** It is much easier to train new team members when systems are in place. Even the training process itself can be a system.

   In my podiatry business I have a 20-day training program in place for all new team members (reception and podiatry). I have a checklist that I follow, which lists activities and duties that must be achieved within a particular timeframe. As each task is achieved I tick it off the list. New and existing team members are unaware this system exists – but it is a very important system for me as the business owner.

7. **Consistency:** I believe this to be the most important reason for having formalised and well-developed business systems.

THE IMPORTANCE OF CONSISTENCY

Consistency means being reliable and dependable and maintaining a constant profile and level of service. *Consistency* may not always be noticed, but *inconsistency* will be noticed every time. *Consistency* is about being *"the best you can be"* on a consistent basis. It's not about trying to copy someone else's level of service that you cannot possibly replicate.

Being consistent doesn't mean you have to be outstanding.

"Hang on, hang on, why can't we be outstanding?"

Well, you can be outstanding if you want, as long as you can be outstanding on a consistent basis. But if you think about it, if you can be outstanding every day, without compromise or error, then this is really your level of consistency, because it is *"the best you can be"*. If you cannot be outstanding on a consistent basis, you need to dial it down a notch and be *"the best you can be"* on a consistent basis. I would much rather receive a consistent above-average service from a business every time I visited them than receive awesome service one day and poor service the next. When you're treated poorly after being treated well, you notice it – and so will your patients. I've visited businesses and have been offered a coffee on the first and fourth visits, but not offered coffee on the second, third and fifth visits, and yes I noticed it. In contrast, I've been to other businesses that have never offered me a coffee, and funnily enough I don't expect it, but the rest of their service is consistent.

PEOPLE FOLLOW SYSTEMS; SYSTEMS SHOULD NEVER FOLLOW PEOPLE

Having systems takes away the guesswork and allows everyone to concentrate fully on patient needs, not their own needs. When developing systems, never change them to suit one person. If a task requires everyone to do three steps, but you have one person in your team who says they do not like doing step 2 because *"it just doesn't suit them"*, do not change the system to suit that one person unless they can show you a valid reason why the system should be changed.

If it is a valid reason then you could modify the system and create a new system for everyone in the business to follow. This is why employing new people can be fun and rewarding: you're getting fresh new eyes, and sometimes systems do become outdated and need to be shaken up. Also, new team members who have worked elsewhere may have observed some systems that are better than the ones you currently have in place, so you must be open to their positive suggestions.

Eliminating bad habits

You should be aware though that some team members who have worked elsewhere could bring with them some bad habits, which could be in direct conflict with the systems you are trying to introduce or teach. But the good news is *systems eliminate bad habits*.

Some bad habits will be the direct result of working somewhere with no systems. However, some people are just lazy, have no work ethic, and will always take the easy road, so their habits have nothing to do with previous employment but more to do with their attitude towards work. Don't let them fool you into believing that their bad habits are a valid reason to change your current system. This is often identified with constant comments such as, *"At the last place I worked we used to..."*.

If a team member brings an idea to you, listen and then decide if it is worth considering, and tell them you will bring it up at the next clinic meeting for further discussion so you can get opinions from other team members. Doing this shows you are open to change and willing to listen, but you will take a team approach to introduction or rejection of new ideas. This way, if everyone thinks it is a bad idea you can shoot it down as a group, but the person who made the suggestion will still feel they have been listened to.

YOUR SYSTEMS SHOULD BE SEEN AND NOT JUST HEARD

Every podiatry business will have systems to some extent, but usually they are not written down and instead are taught by word of mouth. Learning by repetition and continual re-training can work well as long as the business owner or senior team members are always prepared to make themselves available to answer ongoing and repetitive questions, but a better way is to have all your systems in written format in a set of handbooks and flowcharts to explain the processes.

SYSTEMS AND SUB-SYSTEMS

Every task within your business should have a written system, and the more technical systems will need to have sub-systems created for easier management. All written systems should fit onto one sheet of paper; if it goes longer than this, it's an indication you need sub-systems.

For example, you may have a system titled *Telephone Usage System*, however in its entirety it would be a huge system to learn, with many pages, so it's better managed and easier to teach if it is broken into sub-systems. Below are examples of sub-systems that could be created from the **Telephone Usage System**.

Sub-system: *"How to answer the telephone"*

- How many rings are acceptable before the telephone should be answered?

- How should the telephone be answered?

- Everyone should be saying the same phrase and following a "script".

- The exact wording of the "script" forms part of your system.

Sub-system: *"Identifying patient bookings"*

- What questions should be asked to identify a new general patient or biomechanical patient?

Sub-system: *"Common questions patients ask over the telephone"*

- How much are your consultation fees?

- How much are orthotics?

- Do you treat children, knee problems, bunions, back pain, and so on?

Scripts are very useful when it comes to answering these types of repetitive questions.

The telephone is one of the most powerful pieces of equipment in your business, and it can make you a lot of money if it is used correctly, however if used poorly it can also lose you a lot of money.

IDENTIFYING POOR PERFORMERS

Without systems, team members have an excuse for making ongoing errors. They can easily say they forgot how to do something, or tell you they got busy and overlooked a particular task. Having documented systems in place will eliminate this and also help you identify team members that should not be working in your business.

HOW DO YOU KNOW WHEN YOUR SYSTEMS ARE WORKING?

It's easy to know if your systems are working because your whole business runs without any interruptions. There's no patient complaints, no arguments between team members and no bottlenecks or delays. There is complete harmony in the workplace. Another good sign everything is working well is that you can go on holidays for a few weeks and nothing has changed when you return, except your tan.

However, even when everything is running well, it's still a good idea to test your systems. Occasionally ask team members to explain a particular system to you. Are they still doing it the same as it is documented, or have they gone off track slightly? *Is there a reason for going off track?* If so, review your written document to see if something needs further development or if the team needs re-training. People can move away from a system without even knowing it, especially when it happens slowly. This is why system reviews are essential – especially when things are going well.

> "Show me a business owner holding a golf club at 2 pm on a Wednesday afternoon and I'll show you a business owner who has systems in place."

WRITE SYSTEMS FOR 12 YEAR OLDS

As adults we like to complicate simple tasks so that they seem far more important than they really are, and systems are no different.

They do not need to be overly complicated to be effective. In fact, if a system is really good any 12 year old should be able to read it and implement it without any real concerns.

The hardest part about creating a system is getting started. So to help you out, here is my Four-Step Formula for creating effective systems.

Step 1: Write down how things are done in your business. This may sound very simple, but many business owners never get this far and instead they keep everything in their head.

Step 2: Implement the system, meaning have someone follow your instructions to see if it actually works and makes sense.

Step 3: Review the outcome and evaluate the system's effectiveness – then the final step...

Step 4: Re-write the system.

You should also be reviewing your systems on a regular basis because systems are not static, they are dynamic and should continually be revised.

A common question I've been asked is, *"Why do I need to write something down when it's pretty obvious how it should be done?"* Thinking this way is a common mistake; the more obvious a system seems, the more reason it needs to be written down.

As an example: **How do you make a cup of instant coffee?**

1. Put coffee in cup.

2. Add sugar.

3. Add boiling water.

4. Add milk.

This is a very straightforward system, but because it is so simple it is open to interpretation and can result in some good and bad cups of coffee. Now, what would happen if you asked your 12-year-old son to make you a cup of coffee for you based on the above instructions; how would he go? He would start off with enthusiasm, but then constantly interrupt you for further clarification about the instructions he's been given because it's not clear:

1. How much coffee do you have? Would you prefer a heaped or level spoonful? I noticed there are two different spoons in the drawer – which one would you like me to use?

2. Would you prefer a cup or a mug? Which size mug? I noticed there is a mug that has *"I work with Idiots"* printed on the side – is this your mug?

3. How many sugars did you want? Sorry, but did you mean heaped or level? I just noticed there are sugar pills – are these yours? *Are you a diabetic? Is there a family history of diabetes? Should I be concerned?*

4. Okay, you're not a diabetic, but how much milk would you like?

5. What type of milk? I've noticed you have full-cream, low fat, no fat, skim and lactose-free milk in the fridge. *That's a lot of milk. Are you lactose intolerant? I get a lot of wind myself after drinking milk.*

If you don't have written systems for team members to follow, you will constantly be interrupted throughout the day with meaningless questions, not that much different to a 12 year old asking, *"What milk do you want?"* Are you finding this happens to you already, every single day? Is it driving you nuts yet?

A few years ago I had a similar problem when it came to autoclaving instruments. New team members found it difficult to remember which instruments needed to be bagged together, even though *I thought it was pretty obvious.* So to remove future errors and to make it very simple, we took photographs of the instruments that should be grouped together and also what size autoclave bag should be used. These photos were laminated and placed on the wall next to the autoclave, and all team members were told to look at the photographs if they had any doubts. This one simple system modification – adding a photograph – eliminated this error.

> "Make it a rule never to give a child a book you would not read yourself."
>
> George Bernard Shaw

DEVELOPING YOUR SYSTEMS

So how do you get started writing systems? The easiest way is to just hand write them. It may not be perfect, but this is better than not having them documented at all. You can always have someone type your notes up for you at a later date and make it look good. What matters most is that you get something down on paper for your team to follow.

Once your systems are documented and the people involved in performing these tasks get a chance to evaluate and apply them exactly as they have been documented, only then will holes become apparent. When holes are identified you patch them up as you go, however if there are too many holes you may need to throw the system out altogether and develop a new system from scratch. This is how systems develop, and sometimes you just need to know when a system is no good and when it is time to start again. Even though developing systems takes time and effort, it should be something that is ever evolving within your business.

SYSTEMS ADD VALUE

Any business with good systems in place will sell for more than a business without systems. It will also be easier to sell because the new owners can clearly see how things are done because they're documented.

Your business systems form part of your intellectual property and therefore should be protected. Only the business owner should have access to all systems; other team members only need to have access to systems that are required for their particular duties.

Never leave all your systems in one place, accessible to everyone. How would you feel if a copy of all your business systems was given to your opposition? This can happen if a Podiatrist leaves your employment and sets up in opposition to you, so you need to protect your property. Everyone should be made aware that no parts of your manuals should be copied or taken home without permission.

SYSTEM OVERLAP

As you develop systems you will notice that where one system ends, another one begins. This leads to systems overlapping, which is why some systems will be duplicated in different handbooks and training manuals, because more than one person is involved in completing a particular task. *Following is a simple illustration of system overlap.*

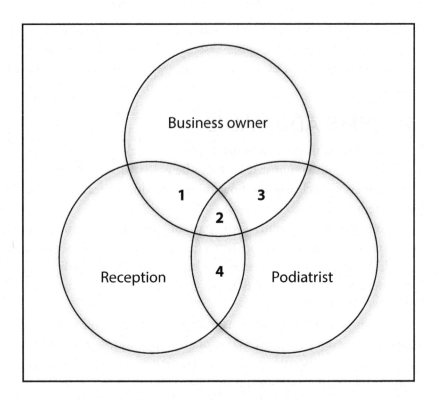

In a typical day there will be systems that will only involve the Receptionists, others that only involve the Podiatrists, and separate systems again for the Business Owner. Then there are the systems that overlap each other. These systems require action from more than one person to achieve a desired outcome.

In this example there are four areas where systems overlap between various team members and the owner. Below are examples of typical tasks that could fall into these overlapping activities.

1. **Systems that involve the Receptionists and Business Owner:**

   ■ Evaluating monthly reports and statistics.

   ■ Discussing upcoming advertising for the month.

I made the mistake once of not informing my Receptionists about an advertisement I had placed in the local paper regarding shockwave therapy. As expected, the telephone went nuts with enquiries about shockwave therapy and my Receptionists couldn't understand why the sudden interest.

2. **Systems that involve everyone:**

   ■ Clinic meetings to discuss how to deal with blowfly patients.

   ■ System changes and updates.

3. **Systems that involve the Podiatrist and Business Owner:**

   ■ Reviewing patient files.

   ■ Discussing treatment plans for various ailments.

4. **Systems that involve the Receptionist and Podiatrist:**

   ■ Patients dropping off orthotics for adjustments.

   ■ Reports being sent to professional referrers in a timely fashion.

   I hate doing reports, so a system has to be in place to make sure I do them, and I expect the same "hounding" from my Receptionists as everyone else. The Business Owner needs to be held accountable just like everyone else.

In larger podiatry businesses with Podiatry Assistants, Lab Technicians and Business Managers, there will be further areas of system overlap.

It's No Secret, There's Money in Podiatry, however...you must have systems.

*After reading this chapter, what ideas are going through your head? Write them down **right now**.*

_____

_____

_____

_____

_____

_____

_____

_____

WORKING ON THE BUSINESS

When your systems are well documented and delegated to the appropriate people it's time for you to start moving onto more important functions within the business. This is referred to as *"working on the business"* instead of *"working in the business"*. This doesn't mean that you have to stop seeing patients if that's what you like to do, it just means stepping back a little.

Working *on*, instead of *in*, your business means you start focusing on the areas of your business that will contribute to long-term growth and expansion, but it doesn't mean that you "have to" do these things. The best thing about working for yourself and being the business owner is that you get to choose what you do, or don't do. Therefore working on your business is a choice.

If you want to have a financially successful business but would prefer to stay as a single practitioner and not employ other Podiatrists then that should be your choice. *Believe me, finding other Podiatrists that you can work with and like can be difficult.* Having your systems documented for your team to follow allows you more time with your patients, or more time with your family at the end of each day, which is a nice choice to have. Many practitioners will spend eight hours a day with patients, then neglect their families for a few more hours because they do not have tasks delegated to their support team.

For those of you who want to employ other Podiatrists and have multiple locations, working *on your business* instead of *in your business* is something you must do. *You do not have the choice.* It doesn't mean you have to give up seeing patients altogether, but your contact time will definitely need to be reduced if expansion and multiple locations are a long-term goal.

You need to work out what works best for you. You have to find your balance between management tasks, business growth and patient contact. For some, giving up complete patient contact works very well, while others need to stay in touch with patients, even if only a few days per week.

SO WHAT IS INVOLVED WHEN YOU WORK ON THE BUSINESS?

Working on your business involves more mental energy than physical energy and involves you paying more attention to areas within the business that are often overlooked and neglected, such as:

- Financial planning – it is easy to overlook your finances, especially when you're busy. More money coming in than going out is not the best financial planning method to use.

- Expansion planning – are you thinking of opening more clinics, or are you thinking of expanding the size of your current clinic? Is it time to renovate?

- Identifying marketing opportunities – you see more opportunities when your mind is free from clutter.

  Seeing patients for eight to nine hours every day is mentally tiring and leaves you with no headspace for creativity. You miss opportunities when you're tired.

- Team development – spending time developing your team will pay dividends.

- Strategic development – what strategies do you have in place to develop your business further? With more free time you can further develop relationships with other health professionals.

- Innovative development – are you always going to do plaster casts or are you going to introduce a scanner? What other cool equipment can you introduce?

- Further system development – there is nothing wrong with constantly developing your systems, but don't introduce a minor change every week or your team will start to get confused. Allow time between system changes so you can test and measure their effectiveness.

- Networking – with more time available to you, you should become more involved in networking opportunities in your area.

Working on your business is not an easy habit to create, especially if you've not done it before. To do it effectively you need to block out time in your diary and you need to commit to it. This is one activity were I would really suggest you get yourself a podiatry mentor or coach because it is so easy to take an afternoon off to work on your business, and instead you end up doing something else. You need to be held accountable to someone other than yourself, on a regular basis.

*After reading this chapter, what ideas are going through your head? Write them down **right now**.*

_____

_____

_____

_____

_____

_____

_____

13

ARE YOU GREEN AND GROWING OR RIPE AND ROTTING?

To learn more about systems I would highly recommend reading *The E-Myth* by Michael Gerber, and anything written about Ray Kroc, the man behind the success of McDonald's. *When you get the chance, Google Ray Kroc, because his story is amazing.* Ray Kroc was once asked why McDonald's was such a phenomenal success, and his answer was very simple: *"We take the hamburger business more serious than anyone else making hamburgers"*, and he was probably right.

- *How serious do you take your own podiatry business?*

- *Did you set it up because it was better than working for someone else?*

- *Are you willing to do what is required to make it a successful enterprise?*

The worldwide success of McDonald's came about by having amazing yet very simple systems. Systems don't need to be complicated to be successful; they just need to have three ingredients:

- They need to be followed by everyone in the business.

- They need to be developed further as the business landscape changes.

- They need to be documented.

Could you imagine McDonald's if Ray Kroc had never spent the time documenting how a cheeseburger should be made? Ray Kroc's McDonald's is run on systems that are so simple; he has been able to create a billion dollar business basically run by kids. These kids can't clean their bedrooms at home and many don't even have a driver licence, however they are an integral part of a billion dollar burger empire. Understanding the power of systems will make you money.

"Are you green and growing or ripe and rotting?"

Ray Kroc

Your greatest growth period in business occurs when you're green, when everything is new and exciting. The problem though is when you stop growing, when you become complacent, settled and happy with what you've achieved. *You've become ripe.* If you don't re-invent yourself and replant new business ideas or change the way you do things within your business, your podiatry business will slowly begin to rot *and smell.*

When a podiatry business becomes ripe, the business owner has three options:

1. Do nothing and eventually rot – this is a poor option, but is not uncommon;

2. Introduce new services and equipment and improve upon the successful formula they already have in place and working; or

3. Expand and open multiple locations.

Options 2 and 3 are good options, however you need to have systems in place and they need to be working well.

*After reading this chapter, what ideas are going through your head? Write them down **right now**.*

_____

_____

_____

_____

_____

_____

_____

_____

YOUR PATIENT
INDUCTION SYSTEM

The aim of having a *patient induction system* is to ensure that first-time users of your podiatry business are greeted correctly and consistently when they arrive, and the key is consistency. When a patient arrives at our business it is important to acknowledge them immediately. It doesn't matter how busy everyone is, it's not too hard to give someone a simple smile to acknowledge his or her presence. There's nothing worse than arriving somewhere and the Receptionist continues to talk on the telephone and does not acknowledge your existence. When you're left hanging, sixty seconds can seem like an eternity.

I have visited a lot of doctor's surgeries and I can't stand Receptionists who peer over their bifocal glasses and, without cracking a smile, sternly say, *"Doctor will be with you shortly, take a seat"*, and then go back to their duties. I get annoyed when I'm treated poorly. I get further annoyed when I'm told the doctor will be with me shortly when I arrive and then I sit there for 45 minutes reading out-of-date, germ-infested magazines.

Nobody asks if I would like a coffee or a glass of water, and I'm not informed how much longer I will have to wait. The message I get from the Receptionist and Doctor is that they do not care about me. What message do you want your patients to receive when they arrive at your business?

Your *patient induction system* is more than just a greeting. If it was just about greeting a patient, this would be called your patient greeting system, but it's not. Your patient induction system is about creating a positive lasting impression, which is what you want your patients to take away with them when they leave your business.

Every patient should complete a patient information sheet, unless you obtained their details over the phone when you made their appointment. If a patient asks why you need all their details, such as date of birth, explain that you need it for identification reasons. If a patient refuses to give you all their information, this is your first indication that you may be dealing with a C or D type patient.

Here's how simple your patient induction system can be:

- Patient arrives: Make sure you greet them with a smile.

- If you're busy with another patient or on the telephone, always acknowledge their presence.

- Have them complete your patient information sheet if this information has not already been obtained.

- Let them know immediately if the Podiatrist is on time or running behind, and keep them updated with waiting time.

- Offer them a coffee, tea or glass of water while they wait.

- If the patient wants to talk and if you do not have other patients to deal with, talk with them. This is far more important than shuffling paperwork and builds good long-term rapport.

- Finally, never discuss personal issues with other team members at the reception desk.

When a patient visits your podiatry business for the first time you want it to be a positive experience, therefore your business should always be bright and inviting, floors should be clean, magazines should be up to date and the overall reception area organised and uncluttered. Sometimes it's the simplest things that leave a lasting impression and make patients talk about your business long after their consultation. Once a week, you should sit in your reception waiting area and look at things from a patient's perspective. Sit in each waiting chair and look around. You will be surprised what you can see, which is often overlooked by the rest of your team who sit on the other side of the reception counter.

Always look for ways to "wow" your new patients. Just having up-to-date magazines in your waiting area may be all that is needed, or magazines that interest men and women.

*After reading this chapter, what ideas are going through your head? Write them down **right now**.*

_____

_____

_____

_____

_____

_____

_____

_____

PART II
MARKETING

15

UNDERSTANDING THE BASICS OF MARKETING

Without marketing your podiatry business will fail, or it will be overrun by younger Podiatrists that do market. Marketing is what distinguishes you from your competitors and it relays a message to your target markets. As a business owner you should constantly be in marketing mode, looking for new opportunities, because business success comes to those that search for it. Internet and social media have changed the way we communicate, think, and how we access information, however regardless of these advancements some fundamentals of marketing have remained unchanged.

TIME AND PLACE

Is there a perfect time or perfect place to market your podiatry business? You better believe there is, and it's *anytime and anyplace.* Opportunities to market your podiatry business are everywhere; you just need to keep an open mind. You can look at other allied health professions and observe how they're marketing in your local area, however don't limit yourself to health care, instead look at the broader market: your hairdresser and the coffee shop across the road, what are they doing that captures your attention? Can you borrow their idea and make it your own?

My local hairdresser, Jan Lyons Salon, offers free wi-fi to every client who has a wireless device and also offers iPads for those who don't, in case clients want to check emails or surf the web while they wait. Children can also use the iPads while their parents are having a haircut. Offering free wi-fi and use of iPads is an inexpensive idea, yet very effective and memorable – but will you implement this idea yourself? I have, and using The Orthotic Economy it only cost my business two orthotics to implement.

CONSISTENCY IN YOUR MARKETING MESSAGE

Regardless of how you market your podiatry business, the most important thing is the *consistency* in your marketing message. If you want to be perceived as the premiere sports podiatry business in your area, you must consistently push that sporting message in all your marketing. You cannot deviate from the message and say, *"…and by the way, I also cut toenails".* This would be a mixed message, and mixed messages in marketing are confusing. Trying to push more than one message also dilutes the main message.

Market one message at a time and only to the target markets you want to attract. If you want to see more sports patients then push that message. If you want more laser treatments for fungal nails, then push that message. This doesn't mean you will never do a nail surgery if you promote sport, but you only have a limited amount of time to capture your audience with your marketing message, so keep your message consistent, focused, and straight to the point. Also, if you want to have a healthy six-figure income, make sure your marketing is targeted towards your services with the highest profit margins and greatest dollar yield per hour.

HELICOPTER MARKETING

Many Podiatrists make the mistake of only marketing their podiatry business when patient numbers are down and business is slow; once business improves they stop all their marketing activities again. This is a very ineffective and inconsistent way to market your business as it destroys momentum. Every time your marketing comes to a complete stop, it takes far more time and energy to get your marketing campaign started again, which is why this form of marketing is referred to as *helicopter marketing*. A helicopter burns far more fuel to get off the ground than it does once it is up and running smoothly through the air. Every time it lands and comes to a complete standstill, it has to once again burn more fuel to get back off the ground.

WHAT IS A MARKETING NICHE?

Earlier we discussed your ideal patient and your perfect target market, or multiple markets, however what happens if you have an interest in sports but so do the other four Podiatrists in your area? If you advertise, *"Special Interest in Sports Podiatry"*, but your competitors are advertising the same message – how can a patient differentiate you? They can't, so you need to create a niche, something that sets you apart from the competition.

For example, triathlons are very popular, and fortunately for Podiatrists, triathlons involve two disciplines we can assist with: cycling and running. If you changed your advertising message from *Special Interest in Sports Podiatry*, which everyone is using, to *We Help Triathletes Reach Their Full Potential*, it would immediately differentiate your business from your competitors. In fact, it still indicates you're interest in sports, but in addition to that, you know more about triathletes than your competitors. If you constantly repeat this message you will be perceived as the expert in that niche, and if I were a triathlete I would visit you over your competitors.

Whoever creates the niche first – owns the niche

To further cement your triathlete niche you would visit every bike store in your area and meet the shop owners, informing them of your expertise in treating triathletes. You would visit triathlon shops and other destinations where triathletes hang out. When you visit Doctors and other health professionals you would mention your experience at treating triathletes. You're slowly starting to own that niche, and whoever creates the niche first – owns the niche.

Why stop there? You could set up a trade display at local triathlon events and offer prizes. Free biomechanical assessments are excellent because only half will ever be used and it costs you nothing. You may even enter a triathlon yourself. Can you see how easy it is to dominate a specific market and create a niche for your podiatry business, and best of all, you don't actually have to have any personal experience in that particular sport; *it's pure perception, but perception is reality*. Your skill and expertise will grow with each patient you evaluate, treat and get back into competition pain free.

> "Very narrow areas of expertise can
> be very productive. Develop your own
> profile. Develop your own niche."
>
> Leigh Steinberg

It's important to note that niches don't have to be sport related. You may create a niche around diabetes and other high-risk foot disorders. You may have an interest is children's foot disorders, laser therapy, shockwave therapy, treating dancers, footwear modifications or orthotics.

What happens if someone already owns the niche you want? If this happens, create a sub-niche. If a Podiatrist has already become a guru in triathlons but you want to be part of that particular sport as well, you simply dig further than they have. You may look at triathletes between the ages of 30 and 55 who are white-collar professionals (high disposable income group), or if you're female, you may target female triathletes. Your only limiting factor when it comes to developing target markets, niche and sub-niches is your imagination.

WHAT ARE YOUR PATIENTS BUYING AND WHAT ARE YOU SELLING?

The general purpose of marketing is to attract new patients to your business, however before you can implement a successful marketing campaign you must first understand what it is your patients are buying and what it is that you are selling. Are you selling what your patients want to buy or are you trying to sell them something they don't want? Many Podiatrists mistakenly think they are selling orthotics to their patients, however this is wrong. Patients don't come to your podiatry business to buy orthotics. Patients come to you to buy *pain relief*, therefore you should be marketing solutions for pain relief and nothing more.

If your pain relief treatment happens to involve orthotic therapy, then so be it, but remember, your number one focus should be selling pain relief because that's what your patients want to buy. Instead of being a salesperson, become a problem solver and help solve patients' problems.

MARKETING IS AN INVESTMENT, NOT AN EXPENSE

When money is tight, the biggest mistake you can make is to cut your marketing budget. It may seem like the most logical thing to do, but it's a mistake. Business Owners tend to look at marketing as an expense, instead of a long-term business investment. You should consider your marketing budget as a fixed cost, just like you would your rent and electricity. However, the amount you invest is not as important as *"the message"* you put out there and the *"consistency"* of when you do it.

As a general rule you should commit a percentage of your gross turnover to ongoing marketing. I have done this from day one and I continue to do so. There are more Podiatrists in Cairns today than there have ever been and my podiatry business has never been busier…so consistent marketing does work.

> "The man who stops advertising to save money is like the man who stops the clock to save time."
>
> Thomas Jefferson

HOW MUCH ARE YOU PREPARED TO PAY FOR A NEW PATIENT?

If you think about it, when you advertise you are basically buying patients for your podiatry business, and your effectiveness in doing this will determine whether you're paying too much or getting them for an absolute bargain. To calculate how much your new patients are costing you, you need to add up all your marketing for the year and divide this total figure by the total number of new patients seen for that year; this will give you your *new patient acquisition cost*.

For example, if you invested $30,000 in marketing in the previous financial year and your business treated 600 new patients in that same period, your *new patient acquisition cost* would be approximately $50 per patient. You must keep this figure in mind every time you're with a new patient and remember that you just paid $50 to have them sit in front of you. *Were they worth it, or were they a blowfly?* If you have employees, you need to inform them about how much each patient costs and they need to respect their value.

You will also come to learn that you don't make much money on a new patient's first visit. If your initial fee was $100 and it cost you $50 to buy them, you've made a gross profit of $50. But this does not take into account rent and other running expenses, and if you have employees, well you're making very little – if anything – on a new patient's first visit. Your profits come from their next visit and the one after that. This is why every employee needs to understand the importance of return visits and offering additional services, as long as it is clinically necessary to do so.

It is far more cost-effective to keep your existing patients coming back than it is to try to keep attracting new patients.

It's No Secret, There's Money In Podiatry, however you must understand that marketing is an investment, not an expense.

*After reading this chapter, what ideas are going through your head? Write them down **right now.***

_____

_____

_____

_____

_____

_____

_____

_____

16 WHAT IS YOUR UNIQUE SELLING PROPOSITION (USP)?

This is really important to understand so read it slowly if you need to. Your *unique selling proposition,* better known as a USP, is a *short statement used in all your marketing to get a simple message about your podiatry business and the services it provides across to your potential patients in a matter of milliseconds.*

Does your podiatry business need to have a USP? Yes it does. In an industry such as ours where the general public doesn't know much about podiatry and therefore considers all Podiatrists equally skilled, it is even more important to develop a USP statement to differentiate your business from your competitors. Once you have developed your USP, you need to use it in all your marketing.

YOUR USP HAS TO BECOME SYNONYMOUS WITH YOUR BUSINESS

Your goal is to develop a strong USP so you stand out from the other Podiatrists in your area that do not understand the power of a USP. As soon as a patient sees your USP statement it portrays an important message about your podiatry business and lets them know what it is you do.

For example, there is a small town with four podiatry businesses and they are all about the same size, have good street appeal and good parking. How does a patient decide which is the most suitable podiatry business for their particular needs? Unless they get a recommendation from a friend, they will go online or use a telephone directory, and this is what they may find.

Business A has a USP that says, *"Quality Podiatry without the High Fees"*.

Business B has a USP that says, *"Children's Feet are Our Business"*.

Business C has a USP that says, *"We Help Triathletes Reach Their Full Potential"*.

Business D doesn't have a USP.

Within a matter of seconds these USP statements give you an idea of what each podiatry business specialises in, so depending on the patient's needs they will be attracted to one of these USP statements immediately. I'm sure you would agree with me that Business D, with no USP, is going to be overlooked, not because the patient thinks *"you lazy buggers, you don't have a USP"*, but because the other clinics have a USP which grabs their attention first. Of course if Business D is the closest Podiatrist and the patient doesn't care who they see to scrape the hard skin from their heels then Business D will probably get their business, but from what we've already discussed this type of patient is not your target market, so that's a good thing.

Did you also notice that the USP used by Business C – *"We Help Triathletes Reach Their Full Potential"* – is the example used when we discussed creating a niche? If you were a triathlete, would Business C be more appealing than A or B? Of course Business C would be more attractive, and the patient would travel past Businesses A, B and D to get to Business C, because of a simple USP in their advertising. Your USP statement should reflect not just who you are or what you do, it should also scream, *"This is the type of patient we're chasing"*.

If you pay attention you will notice most larger businesses have a USP and they use it all the time. For example, M&M's *"Melts in your mouth, not in your hand"* is a very clear message. I remember when Smarties was the king of sugar coated chocolate, but the problem was they used to melt in your hands if you held them too long. Then came along M&M's...they looked just like Smarties, but they didn't melt in your hands. When M&M's hit the market in the 1980s I cannot remember if they were cheaper or more expensive than Smarties, but I do remember their USP and I still eat them often, but I can't remember the last time I had Smarties.

If your USP is good and if it's used often enough in your marketing it will become memorable and will set your business apart from the crowd. It is important to remember when you develop a USP that your business must also be able to back it up, otherwise you are not telling the truth. You cannot have a USP that says, *"Orthotics: Designed, Made & Fitted Within 24 Hours, Guaranteed"* if you cannot guarantee a 24-hour orthotic service.

YOUR USP SHOULD ALSO BE REVIEWED

Don't feel that once you have created a USP statement that you have to stick with it forever. Things change, other podiatry businesses catch up, and consumers may be looking for something different. Therefore your USP statement must change as your business develops, but don't change your USP unless you have something better to say. Federal Express have used the same USP for as long as I can remember, *"When it absolutely, positively has to be there overnight"*, so unless you can say it better, leave it alone.

The USP statement, *"Orthotics: Designed, Made & Fitted Within 24 Hours, Guaranteed"*, is my USP statement at Proarch Podiatry. It was developed to replace my old USP statement, which was *"Keeping Active Feet Healthy"*.

I made the change because:

- it reflects more about what my podiatry business does and the fast service it offers more clearly

- it differentiates my podiatry business from my competitors, who cannot provide orthotics within 24 hours

- my old USP was not really a USP; it was more of a slogan or tagline.

HOW DO YOU DEVELOP A USP?

To develop a powerful USP for your podiatry business you need to bring together information you know about your business with what you think your target markets are looking for:

- What does your podiatry business do that no one else is currently doing?

- Can you improve or provide a service better than your competitors?

- Can you provide a faster service (24-hour orthotics)?

- Do you have a more specialised service (a niche)?

- Do you consistently run on time, which is important for busy people?

To make developing your USP easier, imagine you're the patient – what are your needs and wants when you see a health professional? Is running on time more important than price? For most of us time is money, so busy, hard-working patients will pay a premium if you can consistently run on time. If time is not important, the patient may complain about your fees because they are price-driven. Can you see the difference? A patient that's price driven would more than likely be attracted to Business A's USP – *"Quality Podiatry without the High Fees"*.

In the next chapter we're going to develop your CPOD – your *competitive point of difference* – which is the final step towards developing your podiatry "brand". When these last two pieces of the puzzle are put together you will be ready to start developing a marketing campaign that works and gets results. Many Podiatrists want to take shortcuts and refuse to go through this preparation and development process of understanding their business fully, and then they wonder why their marketing campaigns fail. If you don't understand your business, how can you possibly expect your patients to understand your business?

> **"If I had nine hours to chop down a tree, I'd spend the first six sharpening my axe."**
>
> Abraham Lincoln

It's No Secret, There's Money In Podiatry, however…you must be prepared to do the groundwork.

*After reading this chapter, what ideas are going through your head? Write them down **right now**.*

_____

_____

_____

_____

_____

_____

_____

17

WHAT'S YOUR COMPETITIVE POINT OF DIFFERENCE (CPOD)?

What is it that makes you different from your competitors? You can't say you're better because no one will believe you, plus it's an infringement on our Code of Conduct in relation to advertising, therefore you need to point out your competitive point of difference in another way, and there's only four ways to do this. Your four CPOD options are: *Position, Price, Product and Service*. No matter how good you are, some patients will choose the closest Podiatrist based on *Position*, so there's nothing you can do about that – let them go, they may have been blowflies. Therefore that now leaves three options, *Price, Product* and *Service*. I've already expressed my opinion on discounting and trying to compete on *Price*, so that is also eliminated from the equation, leaving only *Product* and *Service*.

PEOPLE WILL PAY A PREMIUM

Research shows that people will pay more for a premium product and service if they are given the choice to do so. This is why prestige cars are still driven, women wear diamonds, Gucci has not vanished, and people still choose to purchase VIP tickets at music, sporting and business events.

In 2012, on a trip to Los Angeles with my family we had the opportunity to visit Universal Studios. The following ticketing options were available; Standard day entry ticket $84, a front of line ticket $169, or a VIP ticket $299. I hate waiting in line, so for the added service of going straight to the front of the queue I was prepared to pay the $169 ticket price. Going to the front of the line and walking past people who had been waiting for 45 minutes was worth every additional dollar paid.

This year, 2014, I've booked another holiday to Los Angeles with my brother and son, and because we are going to visit Universal Studios again, we decided to purchase the $299 VIP tickets. We're choosing VIP tickets for two reasons: 1) we can afford it, and 2) we were given the choice.

In my own podiatry business I have always focused my efforts towards providing a quality product and a consistent service. I have never tried to compete on price and I think my patients appreciate this. For example, I know my initial biomechanical assessment is more expensive than my competitors, but I don't care because I know I also offer far more at the initial biomechanical consultation. I also know I can make orthotics the same day if needed because we have our own milling machine onsite, but most times we offer a 24-hour orthotic service, guaranteed.

What is your CPOD going to be? If you give it some thought you'll be surprised what you can discover about your own business:

- Do you currently provide a service not offered by anyone else?

- Do you have a particular skill or expertise in a unique area of podiatry?

- Do you offer a guarantee on your product?

- Do you have an exclusive product?

- Do you provide a higher quality product?

- Does your product last longer than your competitors'?

- Can you make it more quickly?

BRAND VS PRODUCT

Your CPOD is what makes your podiatry business different; it's what makes you stand out from the crowd and it helps strengthen your *brand positioning*, but to understand brand positioning you first need to understand the difference between a *brand* and a *product*. For example:

- Panadol is a brand and paracetamol is the product.

- Panamax is a brand and paracetamol is the product.

Both brands contain the identical product and both do the same job, but the majority of people still choose Panadol over Panamax because of brand positioning and the perception of higher quality, even though Panamax is cheaper.

So how does this relate to you and your podiatry business? Well, your business name is your brand and podiatry is your product. You may agree or disagree, but all Podiatrists in your area have the identical product, which is podiatry, but what they don't have is your brand name, meaning your business name. This is why your business name holds so much value and why you need to protect it.

I travel to America quite often and a patient I've known for years was aware of this, and she recently asked me how much it cost to bring the Proarch Podiatry concept to Australia. She asked me this because I have created an amazing podiatry brand in my area. She was shocked to hear that it was not a global brand.

I know you may be thinking your podiatry business is completely different to the other Podiatrists in your area, but your potential patients don't have a clue. They assume we all went to university and we were all trained the same way, so it's only logical to think we're all the same, which is why you need to create a brand about your business name. Your brand positioning is the *"perception"* you create in the patient's mind about your brand (your podiatry business) in relation to your competitor's brand (their podiatry business).

What *perception* are you trying to create about your brand?

- The *"most"* technical.

- The *"most"* efficient.

- The *"best"* podiatry business to see if you're a triathlete.

Or are you creating a *perception* that you're the *"cheapest"* podiatry business in town? The magic word here is *perception*, because what someone perceives to be true is their reality. If your patients believe that your podiatry business is the best at something then that will be the message they will share with their friends and family. They will position your brand first before anyone else. Having a strong USP and knowing your CPOD are all simple building blocks that are necessary if you want to take your brand to the number one position in your area.

Where do you think your podiatry business is positioned right now? I know my podiatry business holds the number one position in Cairns, but I must constantly work and market my business to make sure it stays number one, because I know more and more Podiatrists will venture into my market over the next 5 or 10 years, so I can't rest on my past successes.

> "If you don't make things happen
> then things will happen to you."
>
> Robert Collier

*After reading this chapter, what ideas are going through your head? Write them down **right now**.*

_____

_____

_____

_____

_____

_____

_____

18

SEVEN MYTHS SURROUNDING MARKETING

Many Podiatrists still feel that marketing is deceptive, which is a shame because if you want a successful podiatry business you're going to have to learn how to market yourself and your business. Marketing is merely the transfer of information from one person to another person, so if you hate the word *marketing*, replace it with *exchanging information*, because that's all you're really doing.

Below are seven common myths that I believe are holding Podiatrists back from marketing their podiatry businesses effectively.

MYTH 1: IF I DO MARKETING I'LL BE PROMOTING MY COMPETITORS

Yes you will; when you advertise everybody benefits, so get over it and move on. If your competitors do get a piece of the pie, say 10%, from your marketing efforts and you're getting 90% of the pie, does it really matter? I would much rather eat 90% of a pie than have no pie at all. Even though your competitors get a small piece, what they won't get is to own *that space*. What do I mean by *that space?* If you get in first and tell a story and exchange information with your target market, you will own that message…you will own *that space*, and no one can ever take that away from you. Owning *that space* is extremely powerful and it also helps build your brand.

If another podiatry business tries to tell the same story, your target market will be aware that they are just trying to copy you and will think of your business first because you own *that space*. Think about this – which burger franchise does breakfast, until 11 am, seven days per week? You know the answer; it's McDonald's. They started advertising breakfasts first, and now they own *that breakfast space*. I know Hungry Jacks (Burger King), KFC and Subway have attempted to move into that breakfast space, but unfortunately it's already taken.

Because I have a milling machine installed onsite and I have been marketing a consistent message for the past few years – that we guarantee to have a patient's orthotics designed, made and fitted within 24 hours – my podiatry business now owns *"that 24-hour orthotic space"* because we got in first and took ownership of it. If anyone tries to copy, it won't be as effective and they will promote my business further. *Soon I will be moving into the one-hour space.*

MYTH 2: MARKETING IS JUST ADVERTISING ISN'T IT?

No it isn't. Advertising is one small part of your overall marketing plan. It's like looking at the toes on a foot and saying you're looking at the whole foot.

Placing an advertisement in the newspaper is advertising… it's the toes, but the "message" in your advertisement, the layout, the positioning, your text, the font, the newspaper you select and which day of the week you choose is marketing. Marketing is looking at the whole foot.

MYTH 3: MARKETING IS UNPROFESSIONAL

Yes it can be unprofessional, especially when it is done badly, but how can it be unprofessional to tell a patient that you perform nail surgery when they are considering seeing their general practitioner to have it done? How is it unprofessional to let patients know you are open on Saturday mornings, especially if they live out of town and cannot see you during the week? How can it possibly be unprofessional to let parents know you can help eliminate their son's or daughter's heel pain and have them playing soccer again in no time?

As you can see, it's not the *exchange of information* that is unprofessional; it's how it is done. Offering a patient an inducement is unprofessional, however I believe offering discounts to attract patients is no better.

MYTH 4: MARKETING IS EXPENSIVE

Marketing is only expensive if you don't get a return on your investment. Marketing is an investment, not an expense. To me marketing is a long-term investment in my business and in my family's future. I know marketing works because when I'm at a networking function and I mention another podiatry business in the conversation, I get the same response: "Are there other Podiatrists in Cairns?"

When I arrived in Cairns in 1992 and opened my podiatry business there was one existing podiatry business. I did a lot of marketing in the beginning and have continued to do so, whereas they did zero marketing. I remember one of their Podiatrists saying, *"Unlike you, we don't need to advertise."* Okay, that hurt, but let's move ahead 22 years to 2014 and see where we are. My podiatry business is booming, I'm having record months financially, and the other podiatry business no longer exists. So you be the judge; is marketing an investment or expense?

Marketing doesn't always have to cost you money; some marketing just requires you to invest a little time. Offering advice at a shoe store or organising talks at Rotary and other community events costs you nothing and they should be part of your ongoing marketing commitment.

MYTH 5: MARKETING ATTRACTS BAD PATIENTS

This is not true. Good marketing will never attract bad patients; however bad marketing will attract bad patients, especially if your message is too broad and not focused. If you aim your marketing message at your target market you have far more chance of attracting the type of patient you want at your podiatry business, however if you do happen to get a few blowflies, don't be concerned; send them to a Podiatrist in your area you don't like.

MYTH 6: MARKETING TAKES A LOT OF TIME

Marketing does not take a lot of time, but yes it does take some time and every business owner should be prepared to spend a few hours per week thinking about past, present and future marketing activities. A few hours per week can easily be done after hours and you can do it with or without red wine.

It is extremely important to evaluate your marketing and to be able to gauge its effectiveness, but don't panic, you can have your team assist you. You don't have to do all the work yourself. By getting your team involved you also build team belief in what you are doing. You should also set time aside for brainstorming sessions with your team, because you cannot come up with all the creativity yourself.

If you work by yourself and you don't have a Receptionist, because you feel you cannot afford one, then you need to change this thinking immediately and you need to change it sooner rather than later. Having a casual Receptionist, even if it's only 20 hours per week, totally frees your mind. If you need to, use *The Orthotic Economy to mentally justify the wages you will pay your Receptionist.*

MYTH 7: I'LL NEED TO PAY BIG DOLLARS TO GET A BUSINESS COACH

Once again, not true. Reading books, such as this one, is the first step towards becoming your own expert. Reading books is almost like having a mentor or business coach right there with you. Always make sure you read a book a second or third time, especially if you found it useful the first time.

If the author has a website, as I do (tysonfranklin.com.au), visit it on a regular basis because new ideas are always being developed and posted on these sites. More than likely they will have a blog, and if they have a newsletter, sign up for it, because you can always unsubscribe. The other reason you should visit an author's website is that he or she cannot include every thought or idea in one book – it's impossible. My original transcript for this particular book was well over 60,000 words, so it had to be trimmed, and my website has become the perfect place to store information that didn't make the cut, and some of it is good stuff.

> "Who you are in five years' time will be determined by
> the books you read and the people you associate with."
>
> Charles Tremendous Jones

Coaching itself though is not overly expensive, especially if it gives you a great return on investment. If you do decide to get a business coach, or podiatry mentor, get something in writing regarding the expected increase in revenue from using their services, but be prepared to do some work yourself because it won't all be done for you. A business coach is there to coach you, just like a football coach; they're not there to go out on the field and take the big hits for you.

If a business coach says they can increase your business by 10%, tell them to go away because I think you'll get a 10% increase just by reading this book and visiting my website. If you only want a 10% increase, you don't need to do anything further than apply what you've learnt here. However, if you want more than 10% then you may need a business coach. *Use The Orthotic Economy to justify having one.*

*After reading this chapter, what ideas are going through your head? Write them down **right now**.*

_____

_____

_____

_____

_____

_____

LOOKING FOR YOUR BLACK CAVIAR

Marketing that works today may not be effective tomorrow, and you need to know when your marketing message has become ineffective. One clear sign may be your telephone has stopped ringing, but this doesn't mean your marketing is no longer any good, it just means it may need to be put on the shelf for a while and reintroduced at a later date, especially if it has been proven to work well in the past.

I designed a particular newspaper advertisement in 1998 that is an absolute gem and I still use it to this day, relatively unchanged, because it works every single time I run it. However, after a period of time it starts to become ineffective, and when this happens I give it a spell, just like a good racehorse. This one newspaper advertisement has made my business in excess of a million dollars in the past 15 years, if not more, which is why I refer to this advertisement as my *Black Caviar*. You just know whenever you run it, it's going to be a winner, but eventually it still needs to be rested because all advertising can become tired.

For those people who don't know, Black Caviar is a retired Australian thoroughbred racehorse that created history by being undefeated after 25 races.

BE CREATIVE AND THEN BE BORING

Having a good marketing plan is about being creative and then being boring. This may sound like a contradiction, but let me explain. Once you create a marketing idea that works and produces positive results consistently, you need to just keep repeating it. It may seem really boring, but boring is good, especially if it keeps producing positive results. When it stops being effective and begins to slow, put it on the shelf and give it a spell.

After a period of time, dust it off and use it again. If it produces amazing results again, you've found yourself another *Black Caviar*. I have a radio advertisement that I've been running for at least two years, and my radio rep keeps asking when I'm going to change it because, as she put it, *"It's getting a little boring"*. My response: "I'll change it when it stops working."

TESTING AND MEASURING – MORE NUMBERS TO LOOK AT

So how do you develop a Black Caviar advertisement? Well, just like a good racehorse, it's something you develop over time, and the best way to do this is by testing and measuring. Testing and measuring is a technique used to determine the effectiveness of a marketing idea. In simple terms you test (or *try*) a new marketing idea and then measure the results. Testing and measuring is a process; it's not a destination. It's not an activity you do once and never do again. Just like a racehorse, you don't train it once and never train it again, instead it's something you constantly work on, tweak and improve upon.

For example, if you're thinking about dropping off 5000 flyers in one area with the same headline, instead you can test dropping off five batches of 1000 flyers with five different headlines and see which headline produces the best result. If one particular flyer shines above the rest then you know you have a winner and this is the one you should use again.

Only test and measure one change at a time

With any marketing idea, only test and measure one change at a time. If you change the headline on your flyer, just make that one change and nothing else. Don't change the headline, the text, the layout and the distribution area, because there is no way of determining what change worked best. However, you can test and measure more than one marketing idea at one time. You could be testing and measuring newspaper ads, flyer and direct mail because they are different marketing ideas.

> "Marketing without data is like driving with your eyes closed."
>
> Dan Zarrella

Never use phone activity to indicate the success or failure of a marketing campaign

The number of telephone calls you receive from a marketing campaign does not always equate to a successful campaign. This is also the power of testing and measuring. You may receive a lot of telephone calls from a particular advertisement, but unless those calls are converted to appointments the campaign was not a success. You may receive fewer calls from a different campaign, but if every call is converted to an appointment, resulting in repeat business and further referrals, then it was a successful campaign.

The type of patients you attract can also indicate if a campaign was a success or failure. If you wanted to attract more sports patients, yet you attracted more general patients, then you definitely need to look closely at where and when you are running your campaign and also your message. When this happens, something definitely needs to change.

Your goal with marketing is to eliminate losing campaigns and find winning campaigns. When you find winners, run them again and again, and if they continue to be winners, you may have found another Black Caviar.

It's No Secret, There's Money In Podiatry, but you have to develop some Black Caviars.

*After reading this chapter, what ideas are going through your head? Write them down **right now**.*

_____

_____

_____

_____

_____

_____

_____

20

BEWARE, THERE'S A SALES REP COMING TO SEE YOU

Have you ever considered swimming in a pool of sharks without a safety cage? Probably not, but this is exactly what you do when you begin to advertise. You will attract the attention of many Sales Representatives from various media outlets, all wanting to sign you up as a client. Now, I'm not saying all Sales Reps are sharks, however they will begin to circle like sharks when they become aware of fresh blood in the marketing waters. All Sales Reps pay close attention to their opposition media outlets, so if you begin your advertising campaign by placing an ad in the local newspaper, expect a call within weeks, if not days, from other local newspaper and magazine publications in your area. This will be followed by local radio and television Sales Reps, and so on.

Here's an important tip: if you've been advertising for some time and you're not being circled by other Sales Reps then your current advertising message or medium does not work.

NEVER SIGN ANYTHING ON THE FIRST MEETING

If a Sales Rep says you need to sign today to get a particular deal, just walk away and tell them you need time to consider their proposal, because a good deal today should be a good deal tomorrow. I've rarely seen a marketing proposal that couldn't wait at least a week or two. At your first meeting you want to send a strong message to the Sales Rep that you're not an easy target and you're not simply fresh meat floating in murky marketing waters. This is when advice from a mentor or business coach can be quite valuable.

Basically you need to give yourself time to weigh up the positives and negatives of any proposal and also look at the financial implications for your business. More importantly, you need time to formulate a list of questions so you are prepared for your second meeting with the Sales Rep. *Yes that's correct, you will have a second meeting, because you're now going to tell them what it is you want.*

If you sign an agreement too early you may have missed a perfect opportunity to negotiate for added extras, not mentioned in the first meeting. For example, if a Sales Rep wants you to advertise for four consecutive weeks in the local newspaper, insist on editorial space. If they say this is not possible, tell them editorial space would have been beneficial and sealed the deal, but now you're not sure if advertising in their newspaper is right for your business. *Believe me, you will get the editorial space.*

Every Sales Rep has room to negotiate, regardless of what they tell you. Every Sales Rep has a monthly budget they must meet, so sometimes there can be some good deals available, you just have to be prepared to ask. If they won't budge on price, you may be able to negotiate other benefits such as free tickets or an invite to a sporting or networking event. I have become good at looking for deals for my podiatry business and also working on incentives for myself, my family and for my podiatry team. We often receive tickets to movie premiers, lunch invitations, invites to corporate boxes at sporting events, corporate golf days, and restaurant and travel vouchers.

Even though the benefits from advertising may be great and a lot of fun, the bottom line is you want to generate business. This must be kept at the forefront at all times and this is something that your Sales Reps should also be reminded of, because occasionally they will come to you with a proposal that is complete rubbish and has little benefit to your business. If this happens too often, it's time to move on because they are starting to take you for granted and they are not listening. A good Sales Rep should understand your business, your target market or markets, and also what motivates and interests you.

HAVE YOU ANY IDEA WHAT I DO?

When a Sales Rep meets with you for the first time, let them talk and then politely ask, *"So, do you know what a Podiatrist does?"* Wait quietly for their response. You're not trying to trick them, merely finding out their knowledge of podiatry, which is important if they have approached you with an specific advertising proposal, not vice versa.

If their perception of podiatry is toenail cutting then that's the proposal you will be presented with, however if they think you work with elite sportspeople then the proposal *should be quite different.* Notice I said *should be quite different*, but in reality the advertising proposals placed in front of you will be generic, because they haven't a clue what it is we do, so they're covering all their bases. Often they will tell you this type of broad advertising is called "branding". Be honest and tell them you don't want branding, you want results.

DEMOGRAPHICS

Demographics are the quantifiable statistics of a given population, which when used in marketing can be very powerful, because this information helps reduce the costs of wasted marketing as it helps you become more targeted. If a Sales Rep tells you they have a particular product that is absolutely perfect for your demographic, you should ask them, *"So tell me, what is my demographic?"* You'll learn they have no idea, but this is not surprising considering you've already learnt they have no idea about podiatry, as we've already discussed.

So not only do you need to educate them about podiatry, you need to also educate them on who your "target market" is. This Sales Rep should leave and come back to you with a new proposal. Don't tolerate proposals that have not been properly thought through.

REACH VS FREQUENCY

Reach and frequency are terms often used by Sales Reps to assist in selling their marketing product. Basically *reach* is the number of people that will see your marketing message, whereas *frequency* is about how many times they will see it.

So here's the million dollar question: is it better to make contact with 80 potential patients one time (*reach*), or is it better to make contact with only 20 potential patients four times (*frequency*)? A Sales Rep will tell you that they are both as important as each other, however they are completely wrong because:

Reach without frequency = Wasted money

Marketing is about building a long-term relationship with your potential patients. This is why it is important for your marketing message to be consistent and repetitive, to the point of almost being boring. The more often you share your marketing message with a potential patient – the frequency – the more chance you have of them responding.

One advertisement in a newspaper, with a large distribution, is a waste of money. Yes, I'm sure you will receive telephone calls on the publication day, especially if you have a really strong message, but you will receive a better response if you run the same advertisement numerous times.

Think about this: have you read the newspaper today, or did you watch television yesterday? If so, can you recall any advertisements? Only advertisements with *frequency* will be remembered, the others will be totally lost, unless of course they were unique and made you laugh, or you just happen to be the perfect target market and the message spoke directly to you.

To give you a good example of frequency; there's a business in the Atherton Tablelands called Golden Drop Winery, and they have been advertising on television for years. I think I could almost repeat their television commercial verbatim because I have seen it so many times, but here's the kicker: I don't think I have ever seen their television commercial on before 11 pm. Advertising on late night television is cheap, and because it's so cheap they can repeat their television commercial over and over again.

Now if they went for reach they could have advertised during *The X Factor*. The only problem would have been their budget; it would have been blown after one or two commercials. Reach is very expensive, whereas frequency is inexpensive, but you need to find the happy medium between the two.

Here's an analogy for you to consider: imagine a farmer with 500 fruit trees. The trees need to be fertilised twice each year for them to produce fruit, but he only has enough fertiliser to fertilise them all just once. What should he do? Does he put fertiliser on all 500 trees once (reach), knowing it will produce zero fruit, or should he only fertilise 250 trees twice (frequency), knowing it will produce fruit on 250 trees? Of course the farmer will do option two as fruit from 250 trees is better than no fruit from 500 trees.

So the next time you're considering doing a letterbox drop, instead of having ten thousand flyers delivered once (reach), consider only delivering two thousand flyers, but repeat it five times in the same area (frequency). This also gives you a chance to Test and Measure different headlines, therefore it's a double bonus.

FIVE WAYS TO WASTE MONEY ADVERTISING

Some advertising is just rubbish – it's that simple. Does it mean that you will attract no new patients using these methods? No it doesn't, but you'd be better off investing your money elsewhere. Here is my top five money wasters that should avoided:

1. Drink coasters and score-cards at bowls clubs.

2. Small whiteboards handed out by doctor's surgeries and pharmacies.

3. Community televisions (the silent TVs you see in doctor's surgeries).

4. New magazines in your area that have no readership.

5. One-off magazines for special causes (or they sound like special causes).

BEWARE THE CON

If you're approached with an advertising proposal over the telephone, always request information via email and ask for a contact number so you can call them back and verify their existence.

My Receptionist received a telephone call from a Police Officer wanting to urgently speak with the business owner. Well, of course they got me because it was the Police. When I got on the telephone he quickly explained it was not a Police matter, so there was no need to be concerned. Instead, he was calling to find out if I wanted to advertise in the local Police Journal.

I had come highly recommended, but he couldn't recall the officer's name (*of course not because he was making it up*). After his long speech he informed me I could pay via credit card, over the telephone. I asked if he could email me the information so I could think about it and he said he couldn't because he didn't have an email account (*that's odd*). He also couldn't fax the information because he didn't have a fax machine, and finally he couldn't give me a return telephone number because he wasn't sure what the number was. When I asked which station he was located at, he hung up. *Yes*, it was a con, but I was very aware.

BUILDING RELATIONSHIPS

Don't get disheartened, not all Sales Reps are trying to rip you off; some are honest people with a good product, and eventually you will develop close, trusting relationships with many of your Sales Reps as they get to know you and your podiatry business. In fact, over time many will become close friends, and the long-term development of these relationships is an integral part of your overall business success and future expansion, if that's what you want to do.

*After reading this chapter, what ideas are going through your head? Write them down **right now**.*

_____

_____

_____

_____

_____

_____

_____

_____

USING MARKETING PILLARS TO CREATE BUSINESS STABILITY

Creating a successful marketing strategy involves many factors, and the most crucial of all is making sure your podiatry business has as many referral sources as possible, meaning it has many ways of attracting new patients. It's dangerous to rely on just one or two predominant referral sources, because no matter how good they are, if one disappears, so does half or all your income. Instead, you should have dozens and dozens of referral sources, which when grouped together become what I call a *Marketing Pillar*. A pillar is basically a supporting structure that props up another object; in this particular case your Marketing Pillars are used to support and prop up your podiatry business.

In 438 BC in Ancient Greece, the Parthenon was built. If you ever see a picture of this amazing structure you'll notice the number of large pillars used to support its massive ceiling, and after 2500 years it is still standing and a recognisable structure today.

You need to look at your podiatry business in a similar way; YOUR BUSINESS is the ceiling and your referral sources – when grouped together – are the marketing pillars. There are six Marketing Pillars that should be created for your podiatry business: Professional, Non-Professional, Internal, External, Verbal and Web-Based.

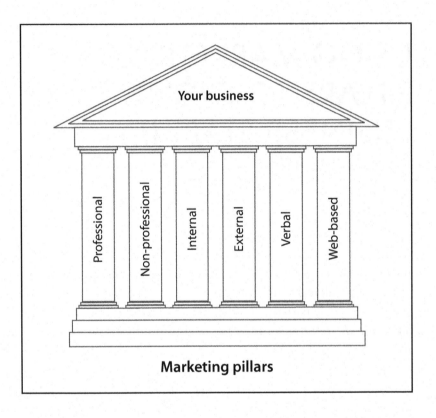

There are also no limits to the number of referral sources you can develop within each Marketing Pillar, and the more you develop, the further it strengthens and stabilises the Marketing Pillar. Also, the stronger the Marketing Pillars, the less chance you'll notice a financial downturn if one referral source, within a pillar, suddenly crumbles. You should constantly be nurturing and maintaining your referral sources and also be adding new referral sources to each Marketing Pillar, for further stability.

So how do you group your referral sources into Marketing Pillars? I don't think there is a right or wrong way to do this as long as it makes sense to you, however here is an example of how I group my referral sources together into Marketing Pillars:

- **Marketing Pillar One: professional referrers:** This comprises all marketing activities that involve Doctors, Physiotherapists, Chiropractors, Osteopaths and other health professionals.

- **Marketing Pillar Two: non-professional referrers:** This group comprises footwear stores, health food shops and other local businesses.

- **Marketing Pillar Three: internal marketing:** This involves everything you do within your business that the general public does not see until they step inside your podiatry business to make an enquiry or become a patient.

- **Marketing Pillar Four: external marketing:** This involves all your visual and auditory advertising directed towards people in your target markets who are not yet patients.

- **Marketing Pillar Five: verbal marketing:** This involves all communications you have with the broader market by way of public speaking engagements, networking events, business lunches, trade shows and the like.

- **Marketing Pillar Six: web-based marketing:** This involves your business website, blogs, and all your business and personal online social pages.

Your Marketing Pillars are the most crucial and important aspect of your business, and because of this I'm going to dedicate a complete chapter to each one, so it can be discussed in more detail.

Some chapters will be longer than others, but don't discount their value based on size. Every Marketing Pillar holds equal importance. This book is all about helping you get your piece of the podiatry pie, so look at your Marketing Pillars as integral ingredients.

> "The aim of marketing is to know and
> understand the customer so well the product
> or service fits him and sells itself."
>
> Peter Drucker

*After reading this chapter, what ideas are going through your head? Write them down **right now**.*

_____

_____

_____

_____

_____

_____

_____

MARKETING PILLAR ONE: PROFESSIONAL REFERRERS

There is a strong correlation between the number of referrals your podiatry business receives and your ability to stay connected with your professional referrers. Your goal is to stay top of mind, because you want to be thought of first, not last, when they're choosing a Podiatrist. The more often you're seen and heard, the more often referrals will flow your way, so be very visible and loud.

Your professional referrers also see the same marketing messages your patients see, so consider your message carefully. Does your message say you're the cheapest, fastest, most advanced, or you're the podiatry business that treats triathletes? Once you start receiving referrals, remember to maintain the relationship because patient referrals you receive today could be gone tomorrow.

CREATING AND MAINTAINING RELATIONSHIPS

Some professional referrers will begin referring to you immediately and then suddenly stop referring. This can happen for many reasons, but the most obvious reason is they've started referring back to the Podiatrist they've used for years. It's nothing against you personally, but a one-off meeting you had six months ago is not going to cement your relationship nor will it break a referral habit. To break this habit, a new habit must be created, which is why you need to stay in regular contact.

But what does it mean if you've been receiving referrals for years and then suddenly they stop? It could mean they're referring patients to a new Podiatrist who made a personal visit to see them; however there can be other reasons.

When I had my podiatry business on the Gold Coast there was a Chiropractor that referred a lot of patients to me, then suddenly he stopped. I was a little concerned, so I went and saw him and asked if there was a problem, and his reason was very simple. He said there was a new female Podiatrist in town and she had big boobs. I gave his answer some thought and concluded I wasn't prepared to get a boob job, so I lost his referrals. The point I'm trying to make is sometimes it's out of your control, but at other times it may well be your fault.

Ask yourself, when was the last time you made contact with your professional referrers? If you can't remember, it was too long ago. Below are some ideas you can start using immediately to stay connected.

Personal visits

Nothing beats a one-on-one meeting with another Health Professional, because it gives you both a chance to put a face to a name. I was surprised how many Health Professionals told me they had never met a Podiatrist before until meeting me. This is also a great time to leave *referral pads, business cards and clinic information brochures* if you have them available.

If you're leaving business cards and clinic brochures in their reception area, make sure you provide your own holders;

otherwise they will probably be thrown out. Also make it a habit to return regularly because if a brochure holder becomes empty it will be removed or used by someone else. *This is why I had my own brochure holders embossed, so they cannot be used by another business.*

After your first visit, rate it out of 10. Write notes about how you felt the meeting went. Was there anything you could have done better? These notes are valuable for your future meetings. Don't be surprised if some of your 10 out of 10 meetings give you no referrals, whereas some 2 out of 10 meetings give you many referrals.

Expected and unexpected patient reports

When a patient is referred, by a professional referrer you will respond with a written report. There is nothing new about this, and this type of report is referred to as an *expected report*. The second type of report though is far more powerful, and is what I call an *unexpected report*, because they don't see it coming.

For example, you see a patient with chronic knee pain and you treat them successfully using orthotics. During their visits the patient mentions seeing their Doctor about the same chronic knee problem and at no stage did they suggest seeing a Podiatrist. When this happens, ask the patient for permission to write to their Doctor about their condition, the treatment you provided and the positive outcome.

Getting permission from the patient will not be difficult, simply ask, *"Do you mind if I write to your Doctor and let them know what treatment we have done, so they have a copy of this in your medical file for future reference?"* Your patient will say yes every time. If you continue the habit of sending *unexpected reports* you will slowly notice an increase in referrals because professional referrers do not want to look stupid for not referring.

Simple emails

You need to gather as many email addresses as possible and add them to your database. Using an email database is an inexpensive way of staying in regular contact with your professional referrers, and it should be updated annually by contacting the Practice Managers. When it comes to sending emails, you need to have a valid reason otherwise you will become that annoying Podiatrist and will be put in the junk mail box. Keep emails simple and stick to the facts:

- Change in trading hours: *We're now open till 1.30 pm on Saturdays.*

- New equipment: *We now have lasers for fungal nails.*

- New services: *We now provide foot acupuncture.*

Email newsletters

Email newsletters can contain more information than a simple email, however they must still be informative, otherwise a professional referrer won't want to read them. Email newsletters are inexpensive and a great way to – for example – promote Foot Health Month and also an opportune time to discuss seasonal sporting injuries, but don't make the newsletter all about podiatry, otherwise it can be boring. Once you start a monthly email newsletter campaign you must maintain it and make sure it is sent about the same time each month.

Even though email newsletters are inexpensive and work well, they can also have limitations if there are many professional referrers in a group practice sharing a common email address. If this is the case, you should try to obtain individual email addresses wherever possible.

Alternatively, it may be worth sending a hard-copy newsletter as well, addressed to each professional referrer. Hard-copy newsletters are statistically more effective than email newsletters, however they're also more expensive and time consuming.

Contact Practice Managers

Are you aware that the Practice Manager makes most of the daily decisions at most clinics? They are the person who decides what brochures will stay and be displayed in the reception area, who is on their referral speed dial and who can and cannot get a meeting. This is why you need to try to build a relationship with the Practice Managers, because they are the Golden Goose.

Taking one Practice Manager to an informal lunch is a great way to build a lasting relationship, but here is an idea worth considering: organise a Practice Managers' Lunch. *Every town has a local business club or something similar that meets on a monthly basis, and they usually have an interesting guest speaker, so these lunches are perfect. Depending on your budget you may only book a few seats to begin with, but ideally you want to book a table of 10 and make sure you take your Receptionist and/or Practice Manager. Getting Practice Managers on your side is almost like insider trading, but a more legal version. Plus, Practice Managers talk to other Practice Managers, so they're great at increasing your word-of-mouth advertising.*

Professional referrers survey

Each year you should send a survey to all your professional referrers. The purpose of this survey is to gather valuable feedback about how you are being perceived by other health professionals and their patients. Your patients may never tell you they have a problem, but they will share it with their Doctor. Don't expect positive comments from everyone, and in fact you want a few negative comments because they give you an opportunity to improve your service. Do not email this survey; it's best to mail or hand deliver it instead, and make sure you enclose a reply paid envelope for its return or schedule a time to return and pick it up.

Acknowledge Australia Day

Professional referrers receive numerous cards and gifts at Christmas time, none of which are remembered, however no one acknowledges Australia Day. I bet if you do you'll stand out from the crowd because nobody else will do it, *until now.*

Acknowledging Australia Day can be achieved by sending a simple Australia Day card, or if you want to invest a little more money you can organise bottles of wine through a corporate wine supplier with personalised labels. I have done this on many occasions; it is an absolute winner and a great way to stay in touch. Don't limit personalised wine labels to Australia Day, you can use them at any time throughout the year. *Warning: make sure you taste the wine because you don't want to send toilet water.*

Third party events

A third party event is where you piggyback off another organisation's event and use it to promote your podiatry business. A great example of a third party event is a charity golf day. It's a simple concept: you enter a team, pay the team fees and invite people you would like to spend four to five hours with. Entering a team can cost as little as $450 and using The Orthotic Economy is less than one pair of orthotics.

Corporate boxes at sporting events work in a similar fashion. When the Queensland Reds Rugby Team played the Crusaders in Cairns I organised a corporate box and it cost me $1500 for the day including food and alcohol, and I was able to invite 10 people. I received over $3000 in referral business the following week, and to this day I still receive referrals from some of the health professionals I invited that day, so it was a great investment.

Information evenings

If you introduce a new service or unique piece of equipment to your podiatry business you should inform all your professional referrers, and the best way to do this is to organise an information evening. When you send out your invites, offer two or three dates and times, because one date and time will not suit everyone, and giving a choice shows you care about having them attend.

Not everyone is going to attend an information evening, which is expected, but by at least sending out an invitation you have not only informed them about your new product or service you have also kept the relationship connected.

Public notices

You should make a habit of scanning the newspaper to see if any new health professionals have recently moved to the area, and if they have you should contact them before anyone else does and send them information about your podiatry business. You should also try to organise a one-on-one meeting as soon as possible.

Opening party

If you're opening your first podiatry business, make sure you have an opening party. Don't let this opportunity slip past. You should invite every professional referrer you have met personally, and close friends and family, and really enjoy the night. Also invite the business editor of the local newspaper and any local magazine editors. But don't limit celebrations to just your opening. If you renovate, expand or relocate, this is reason enough to celebrate. You can also celebrate milestones in business. Once again only your imagination limits you, and using The Orthotic Economy a decent party would cost you approximately one orthotic, maybe two depending on the numbers and quality of your catering.

TRACKING YOUR PROGRESS

Keeping all your professional referrer information in one place is paramount, and creating a simple spreadsheet is one of the easiest ways to get started, however there are specific computer programs available for this specific purpose if you feel your database is becoming too large.

Your biggest goal though with tracking your professional referrers is to keep this information accurate and up to date. Over a period of time you will notice patterns starting to form with the amount of contact you have vs patient referral numbers.

*After reading this chapter, what ideas are going through your head? Write them down **right now**.*

_____

_____

_____

_____

_____

_____

_____

23

MARKETING PILLAR TWO: NON-PROFESSIONAL REFERRERS

I define a non-professional referrer as any business or individual that has the ability to refer a patient but would have no need for a referral pad, however they would benefit by having your business cards and clinic information brochures. Non-professional referrer's may include:

- shoe stores

- sporting stores

- pharmacies

- gyms

- personal trainers

- masseuses

- health food shops.

However, don't limit yourself to the most obvious businesses; think outside the square. What about:

- coffee shops

- hairdressers

- real estate offices

- beauty salons

- hotel and motel service directories – *I've heard people on holidays still have foot problems*

- law offices – *they pay very good money for your podiatric opinion*

- banks, airlines, accounting firms – *many large companies will pay you hundreds of dollars to come in for an hour and speak about foot health. You just need to sell yourself and the benefits of foot health and how it relates to work, health and safety.*

TREAT THEM EQUALLY

You should treat your non-professional referrers with the same respect as you would your professional referrers – they deserve nothing less and they must be nurtured in a similar fashion. You should:

- add their details to your email database

- know the names of the business managers

- send an Australia Day card and bottles of wine

- get involved in third-party events

- invite them to lunches

- invite them to information evenings and parties.

If you have to ask yourself if someone should or should not be added to your list of non-professional referrers, then the answer is yes.

You need to maintain regular contact with your potential non-professional referrers, but don't try to shove podiatry down their throat. Don't ask if you can leave business cards straight away; wait until you're on a first name basis and then politely ask if they would mind if you left some business cards at some point in the future. If they say yes, don't immediately pull them out of your bag; instead tell them you'll bring some cards the next time you're in the area. If you build a good relationship with them, they may ask you for business cards before you get a chance to offer.

"A person's a person, no matter how small."

Dr. Suess

SHOE STORES

For obvious reasons shoe stores should be our greatest non-professional referral source, therefore you should visit every shoe store in your area and try to meet the storeowner or store manager. Once again, unless they ask you for business cards upfront, I would not offer them immediately. Just wait a while. You should assume they already work closely with a Podiatrist in your area, but don't be shy – ask them up front which podiatry business they currently refer to and why.

It could be they've never had a choice before because there was only one Podiatrist in the area...but now that they do have a choice you could be the one. On the other hand, their chosen Podiatrist may be their brother, in which case you stand no chance, but knowing this information up front will save you a lot of time and money.

If they say they don't work with anyone, immediately offer in-house training for their staff. Let them know the better educated their staff are, the more footwear they will sell (plus you'll get more referrals). If they say no then they probably do work with a Podiatrist but didn't want to admit it. You could offer your services once a week or once a month, for free foot screenings and customer advice. If you do, always schedule this after hours, on Thursday nights or weekends, so it does not interfere with your own clinical hours.

Most importantly, make sure the relationship is reciprocal and not all one-way traffic, which can be the case with many storeowners. They will take, take, take, and give nothing in return. You'll offer your services every Thursday night for free, and when it comes time to buy a pair of shoes for yourself they give you a 10% discount. If you're also providing in-house training with their staff you should be able to leave your business cards on display at the front counter; if not, you need to move on and build a relationship with another store. You should also be getting regular referrals from their store. If this is not happening after a few weeks, once again you need to move on and put your efforts elsewhere. Don't let anyone take advantage of you and your expertise. Remember,

*It's No Secret, There's Money In Podiatry, however...*there needs to be a return on your efforts.

*After reading this chapter, what ideas are going through your head? Write them down **right now**.*

_____

_____

_____

_____

_____

_____

_____

_____

MARKETING PILLAR THREE: INTERNAL MARKETING

Is there any better time and place to educate your patients and promote the vast services your podiatry business has to offer than when a patient is sitting in your waiting area or treatment chair? I don't think so. However, after their initial visit, you do have all their contact details in your patient database, meaning you can continue to promote your services well into the future. A large patient database is gold, and you should constantly be trying to add names and grow this database list. Your whole internal marketing strategy revolves around your patient database, so never archive a name unless the patient dies or they move away.

I still kick myself today for deleting over 15,000 patient names from my database, between 1992 and 2006, because I didn't understand the power of developing a good patient database. As you read through this chapter you'll understand why I should never have deleted these patients, but we all learn from our mistakes – and I confess I have made plenty of them.

Internal marketing is about practice development and commitment to improving your patients' service experience, which leads to long-term business success. You should constantly be promoting your services and treatment options, and internal marketing is how you do it. If you choose not to educate your patients, don't be surprised when they go to another podiatry clinic for other treatment. Never assume they know about all the services you provide.

Many years ago a close friend of mine brought his daughter in to replace her old orthotics. She sat down and immediately I noticed a bandage on her big toe. I asked if she kicked it and he said no, she's just had nail surgery from a local Doctor. When I asked why he did not bring her to see me for the surgery, he said he thought I only did orthotics. In contrast to this, I had another patient who needed orthotics, and after fitting them I made a comment about her callused heels and she said she was overdue to see her Podiatrist for treatment. I asked why she didn't see him for orthotics and she said she didn't think they were qualified to do that type of work.

Both these stories demonstrate why we need to educate our patients constantly and why you should never assume they know what we do. Internal marketing is only limited by your imagination. Below are some internal marketing ideas you should implement over the next few months if you're not already doing so. *They are definitely not in order of importance, and this is not a complete list of ideas – it's endless.*

FLAT-SCREEN TELEVISIONS

You should have a flat-screen television in your reception area, because it's a perfect opportunity to promote all the services you offer. You could have a DVD created by an audio-visual professional, or you could create something yourself. There are many apps and inexpensive programs available that can assist you with this process. Recording and editing on your iPhone is fine, as long as you can get the lighting and sound right. If you don't have a television in your reception area, what are you doing?

Does this mean you should never show free-to-air television? Well, it should be limited as much as possible. The midday movie adds nothing to your business and can be quite distracting, however when there is a special event, such as the Aussie Tennis Open, Cricket, Olympics, Super Bowl or even the Academy Awards, you probably need to have it on, but at all other times use it to promote your business and the services it has to offer.

PATIENT INFORMATION FOLDERS

A patient information folder is a loose sleeve folder that contains copies of all your editorials about common foot ailments and services you offer. You should have at least two folders in your reception area at all times, and on a regular basis you should rotate the order of the articles, or write a new article and place it into the front of the folder, to keep your patients interested. All your editorials should be on your website, so you can print them in colour, directly from the website, which will give your folder uniformity and a feel of familiarity if patients visit your website afterwards. Make sure your patients are aware that these editorials can be downloaded from your website, if they need more copies for family or friends.

The patient information folder can be placed with your other magazines, but what I like to do is place it on one of the reception seats, so patients have to pick it up to sit down, which increases the likelihood of them reading it. If the patient puts it back with the magazines, it should be put back on the seat again when they leave.

PUT UP SIGNS THAT SAY "WE HAVE A WEBSITE"

In your reception area and in every consultation room you should have a sign, in full colour, mentioning your website, and other social media sites your podiatry business is involved with. *Please Like, Follow and Review us on:*

If nothing else, it will create conversation and drive more people to these web-based areas. Tell your patients the benefits of *liking* your social media pages, and if they're not sure what to do, give them instructions. Even better, hand them an instruction sheet on exactly how to do it because each social media site has a slightly different process to follow, so you should become familiar with each site yourself.

PICTURES AND POSTERS ON YOUR WALLS

If it's not relevant to you, your family or your business, take it down. Ideally posters on the wall should be promoting other services you offer, or reflect something about you, and never put anything on the wall unless it is framed. If you're using sticky tape or Blu-Tack you should slap yourself. Picture frames where posters can be snapped in and out are perfect for internal marketing, because you can change the posters on a regular basis, and having one-off posters printed is quite inexpensive. If you store them correctly they will last for years.

Information posters should not be limited to your reception; you can have them in every consultation room, on backs of doors and also in the toilet. You could be quite humorous with your toilet poster if you wanted to – *"now that you're seated and we have your full attention…"*.

(Note: A and B type patients appreciate good, light-hearted humour.)

CLINIC BROCHURES

Clinic brochures are an easy way to put all the services you provide into one simple document, and you should hand one to every patient that enters your podiatry business. You do not need to do a massive print run initially, instead use the services of a graphic artist to help you get the design right, then go to the printers and have it professionally printed, in colour. You don't need thousands to get you started; just a short run of 150 or 200. Or, you can print them yourself if you have a good-quality laser printer. Never photocopy a clinic brochure if you're running low, as a poor-quality copy will reflect poorly on your business.

All brochures should be placed in brochure stands and they should be easy to access. Depending on your target market, every general patient should be informed about your biomechanical services and every biomechanical patient should be informed about your general services. Give them a brochure!

If you have the space, write a brochure for each of the services you provide, in addition to your overall clinic brochure.

PATIENT RECEIPTS

Every patient should be given a receipt, so why not print your receipts onto pre-printed flyers promoting another service that your business has to offer? The flyer can be black and white, but colour is far better. You could have more than one flyer and vary it based on the type of patient receiving the receipt. For example, a general patient needs to know more about your biomechanical services and your biomechanical patients need to know more about your shockwave, acupuncture and nail surgery services.

Why not use the same idea – printing onto pre-printed flyers – for all your correspondence? You could use it for all patient letters and podiatry reports to professional referrers.

INTERNAL MARKETING SURVEYS

Every podiatry business wants more A and B patients, but how do you find them? One of the best ways is to create an internal marketing survey and ask your patients simple questions. You don't need a separate survey sheet for each patient. I would suggest you formulate a list of questions on one page and you just put a mark next to each question when you get a response, creating a simple tally sheet. For example:

- What radio station do you listen to?
  - o local radio stations
  - o national radio stations
  - o I don't listen to the radio

- What times do you listen to the radio?
  - o mornings
  - o during the day
  - o drive time

- What do you watch on TV?
  - o Which TV stations (free to air TV or pay TV)?
  - o What are your favourite programs?

- What do you read?
  - newspapers:
    - local
    - national
    - free weekly
  - Do you read locally published magazines?
- Do you still use the telephone directory to find a business or do you prefer to search online?
  - How do you search (Google, Bing, Yahoo, Yellow Pages Online, etc.)?

This information is extremely important when it comes to planning your future marketing, as you want to maximise your results by only attracting your target market, which is more A and B patients and fewer C and D patients. The results from your surveys will sometimes be the exact opposite to what your Sales Rep is telling you about their marketing product.

I had a Sales Rep from a locally published FREE magazine visit me and they explained how good their publication was and why it would be perfect for my podiatry business. Fortunately, I had already started my internal marketing survey and found that none of my A and B patients bothered reading this FREE magazine because it was rubbish; however, patients that were identified as being C and D patients did read it and looked forward to it each month. Isn't that interesting?

ON-HOLD MESSAGES – YOU NEED THEM

When a patient is placed on hold it can seem like an eternity, and if you're forcing them to listen to Richard Clayderman against their will it can seem even longer and is just plain mean – *unless of course you own a piano shop.* As an alternative, you could have the local radio station playing, but what if your competitor is advertising on the radio station at exactly the same time? You could lose that patient. As an alternative, you should consider having an On-Hold messaging system. Actually, you shouldn't just consider it… you should have it.

On-hold messages give your podiatry business a very professional, corporate image, which cannot be underestimated. Even as a sole practitioner you can create an image of being much larger than you really are. Remember: *perception is reality.* On-hold messages give your podiatry business a perfect opportunity to market to both new and existing patients.

If a patient or potential patient has to be put on hold for 60 seconds, why not tell them about your podiatry business in more detail? Tell them about the vast range of services you offer and the new services you've recently introduced. I've had many patients ask for more information about one of the messages they've heard while being on hold.

I did not plan on endorsing any particular company when I started this book, however I have used the services of 1800 ONHOLD since 2003 because they are very good at what they do, which is why I don't mind giving them a plug. I met the owners, Troy and Sue Cooper, when we both won our respective categories at the Telstra Queensland Business Awards, and their enthusiasm towards their product totally blew me away. We have been clients ever since. Prior to meeting Troy and Sue, I was under the illusion that only large companies could afford a personalised on-hold messaging system, but this couldn't have been further from the truth. In reality, it is a very cheap marketing product that you should introduce.

Another benefit of on-hold messages is your messages can be updated and changed throughout the year quite easily, at no extra charge. This is important because your business is constantly evolving, so you want your messages to evolve with your business.

ANSWERING MACHINE MESSAGES

Answering machine messages should always be short and to the point, and once again you have a captured audience so it's a perfect opportunity to leave a good first impression. Below are two answering machine messages. You determine which one sounds better:

- **Example one:** "Hello, you've called Proarch Podiatry. Our clinic is currently unattended so please leave your name and telephone number after the beep and we will return your call as soon as possible. Thank you."

- **Example two:** "Hello and welcome to Proarch Podiatry. We're unable to answer the telephone right now, but would love the opportunity to return your call to discuss how we can be of service to you. After the beep, please leave your name and telephone number and one of our friendly team will get back to you as soon as possible. Once again, thank you for calling Proarch Podiatry and we will be in touch with you shortly."

Can you see the difference between the two messages? There's nothing wrong with the first message, however the second message is by far more professional and shows a more appreciative attitude towards receiving the telephone call, because you *do* appreciate their telephone call – it's not a burden or interruption.

If you're planning to be closed for an extended period of time, outside of the normal public holidays, make sure you adjust your answering machine message with accurate and up-to-date information about your closure period. This is especially important over the Christmas holiday period because some podiatry businesses will close only for the public holidays while others will close for the full break over Christmas and New Year. Make sure you inform your patients when you will re-open.

STANDARD LETTERS

Sending a simple letter is still one of the easiest ways to stay in touch with your patients, yet it is often overlooked. A simple *thank you letter*, sent to all new patients after their initial consultation, is the first letter you should introduce. Think about it… when was the last time you were thanked by a business for using their services? I've stayed in a lot of hotels and not once have I been thanked, even though I drop $200 to $300 per night, so does this make me want to stay there next time? Probably not, unless the hotel itself was exceptional, like the Gaylord Hotel and Resort in Nashville, Tennessee.

Look at every letter as an opportunity to promote your podiatry business further. Your thank you letter shows that you appreciate their business, and it is a perfect opportunity to enclose information about another service you may offer. The idea is to think…what do you do that this patient may not know about? Then supply this information.

In my podiatry business I use approximately 20 different standard letters for various reasons. Some are recall letters, others are re-activation letters, and then I have standard letters designed to promote specific services and special offers throughout the year. These letters constantly evolve as my business evolves, and my patient database determines what letters are sent and to whom. The bigger the patient database, the more letters you can send, meaning the more response you will receive…meaning the more $$$$ you will make. This is why you shouldn't delete names from your database!

NEWSLETTERS

Whole books have been written about newsletters, so I'll keep this brief and straight to the point. My daughter brings home a newsletter every Tuesday from her school. My wife always reads it because she wants to know what is happening at school, but does she have the same enthusiasm for the newsletter she receives from her Chiropractor? No, because it's irrelevant. The whole newsletter is about the Chiropractor and their business. Occasionally there will be an interesting article, however there's nothing that makes my wife look forward to reading it, so here's the lesson: unless the newsletter has relevance to the patient, it is a waste of time. If you prepare a newsletter, make sure it is all about the patient. Give them a reason to want to keep reading. Make it valid and worthwhile. What's in it for them? This applies to both emailed and mailed newsletters.

EMAILING DATABASE

Using emails to stay in touch with patients is very inexpensive, fast, and an immediate way to communicate with patients about sudden changes within the business. Emailing is far more cost effective than sending mail, however *it's a proven fact that a letter addressed to a patient is far more effective than an email.*

Using email to market to your patients is only effective if it's done properly. If you send too many pointless emails you will be added to the patient's "junk" mailbox. Also, the same rules apply when sending emails to patients as they do when sending emails to professional referrers. You need valid reasons to contact them, such as:

- a change in clinic hours

- closing and opening times over holiday periods

- a new service

- a "special offer".

PATIENT SATISFACTION SURVEYS

Patient surveys are an excellent way to stay in touch with patients and gain valuable information and feedback about your business and your team. Negative feedback should be viewed as an opportunity to improve. One negative comment means nothing, but if the same comment is being repeated then you need to address it, unless they are complaining about your fees. As I mentioned earlier, if you're not getting 10% of patients complaining about your fees then you're not charging enough – so put your fees up.

With any survey, it's important to work out:

- What questions do you want to ask? Your questions will affect the answers.

- Which patients are you going to send it to? Biomechanical and general patients will respond differently.

- When will you send it? Will it be sent after their initial consultation, after their orthotics are fitted, or one week after their treatment is finalised?

You can have more than one survey, and surveys can be sent with other standard letters. *You could send a survey with every new patient thank you letter.* Always allow an area on your survey sheet for further comments from the patients, and make sure you have *reply paid envelopes* enclosed with your surveys.

TELEPHONING PATIENTS

The telephone is time consuming but is still your most valuable tool and should be used for:

- *Confirming patient appointments:* It may take half an hour to confirm every patient booked for the following day and cost you a few dollars in telephone calls, but it is a service patients very much appreciate and also gives you an opportunity to make contact with a patient who had forgotten or had decided not to attend. *I know more and more businesses prefer sending SMS and email confirmations, but I still prefer the telephone because when someone says they can't make their appointment because they're sick, I want to hear the congestion on their chest, and you can't get this with an SMS or email.*

- *To enquire how a patient is feeling after nail surgery:* How do you think the patient would feel if you called them, after hours, to see how they are feeling after nail surgery? I bet your competition doesn't do this.

- *To follow up recall letters:* Why send a recall letter and then leave it to the patient to contact you? All recall letters should be followed up with a phone call approximately one week later.

- *Responding to surveys:* If a patient returns the survey sheet and they have left further comments and a telephone number, you need to call them and respond.

The one big problem with technology is it's given us the ability to communicate badly with our patients, more often, so make sure you use it wisely.

REVIEWING AND REACTIVATING PATIENT FILES

Even with the best systems in place, some patients still manage to fall through the cracks; therefore you should review all patient files on a regular basis. This task is so important you should do it yourself until you have trained another team member to do this for you, but do not delegate this task too early. You need to thoroughly develop your system for reviewing past patient files.

Your goal when reviewing patient files is to look for irregularities and gaps in treatment plans. For example:

- A patient may have used your podiatry business for general foot care every two months for the past five years and then suddenly stopped. Why?

- You look at another patient file and notice the last thing you wrote was for the patient to re-book in two weeks for an orthotic review, but they never did. Once again, why?

- Another patient says they need to check with their wife before committing to orthotics and will get back to you, but they never did. Why?

Once you identify an irregularity, you need to send the patient a well-constructed letter to find out why they have not returned. You could telephone the patient, but a letter gives you an opportunity to promote a new or existing service. This letter should be followed up with a phone call one week later. The more effort you put in now to retain your existing patients, the less money you will need to invest in the future to attract new patients.

KEEP INTERNAL MARKETING CONSISTENT

The most important part of internal marketing is consistency. Your information folders, posters on walls, clinic brochures, patient receipts and all correspondence should be consistent in design, colours and fonts, so it resonates familiarity to your patients. You should have a meeting with all team members *today* and discuss further ways to implement internal marketing.

*After reading this chapter, what ideas are going through your head? Write them down **right now**.*

_____

_____

_____

_____

_____

_____

_____

_____

25

MARKETING PILLAR FOUR: EXTERNAL MARKETING

Internal marketing focuses solely on developing your existing patients' experience and knowledge about your business, whereas *external* marketing encompasses everything you do to attract new patients to your podiatry business. From the time you leave your house until the time you arrive back home again, you should be conscious of the fact that you're in marketing mode. This chapter is going to touch on some of the major areas of external marketing, however this list is far from complete.

START HERE: WORK SHIRTS

Before you do anything else, you need to have a work shirt with your logo proudly displayed. Yes, a work shirt is external marketing, and here's a simple truth: every successful podiatry business has one, and every unsuccessful podiatry business does not. Isn't that interesting? It's important that every team member has a work shirt, and it should be worn every day. There are no excuses for it not to be worn. If I have a day off during the week, I still wear my work shirt.

When you are consistently marketing your business, your business name becomes familiar; therefore a work shirt worn outside of the business gets noticed. How often have you asked a patient where they work? If they wore a work shirt you wouldn't need to, so work shirts can speak on your behalf, like a silent salesperson. I've been practising podiatry since 1989 and I'm yet to have someone ask me a foot-related question when I'm wearing my Nike shirt, but it happens all the time when I'm wearing my work shirt.

If you're opening a new podiatry business, don't wait until you are officially open for business before wearing your work shirts because you will miss countless opportunities. Every person you meet during the construction period is a potential patient.

NEWSPAPER ADVERTISING

Newspapers are such a traditional form of external marketing, however they are also the most misunderstood. Many Podiatrists think placing an ad is simple, however I'm here to tell you it's not. To get the most value from your advertising you need to considered the following:

- Are you advertising in the daily or weekly publication?

- Do you know the "readership"?

- Do you know the readership breakdown per day?

- Do you know the demographics of the readership?

- What section of the paper are you targeting?

- Do you want general, early news or sports?

- Are you going to advertise in a feature section (such as health or business)?

- Do you want the first half of the paper or second half of the paper?

- Are you going to advertise in a lift out (such as the television guide or health guide)?

- Are you going to advertise in a promotional guide (family health guide)?

- Are you doing a display ad or a line entry in the public notices?

- What size display ad will work best?

- Are you aware certain pages are more powerful than other pages?

- What position on the page have you requested?

- Do you understand what loading is?

- What is the content of your ad?

- What is the message?

- Do you know the font and layout affects how people perceive your ad?

- Who is your target market?

- Do you have one clear message or is it a mixed message?

- What is the layout of your ad?

- Did you know your business name should not be at the top of the ad?

- Does the ad have a strong headline?

- Is your ad in colour or black and white?

- Have you considered how your logo will look if not in colour?

- Does your logo lose recognition if it's too small?

- Are you using photographs?

- Are your photographs of high enough quality?

- How frequently will you be running your ad?

- Can you request editorial space?

- Can you create a media release to coincide with your advertising?

As you can see, newspaper advertising is far more complicated than it seems, and this is why some Podiatrists fail with newspaper advertising, because they simply get it all wrong.

MAGAZINES

Advertising in magazines is similar to newspaper advertising, however they will be full-colour and published monthly or bimonthly. Magazines are usually aimed at a specific audience. In Cairns we have many locally published magazines. There are two publications aimed at families with children, one aimed at sports people and another two directed towards women. All of them are free magazines and revenue is generated through selling advertising space, so keep this in mind. If you have similar publications in your area, *beware of sharks*.

Are free magazines worthwhile? Well, this really depends if the magazine fits your target market. Anytime a magazine is free it does hold less value and can therefore be picked up and read by anyone, especially C and D type patients who love freebies. However, magazines that are not free hold more value and therefore will be read by potential A and B type patients.

MEDIA RELEASES AND EDITORIALS

Have you ever considered why some Podiatrists appear regularly in the newspaper and you don't? The answer is simple; they submit regular media releases and editorials with high-quality content. They don't wait for media outlets to contact them; instead they actively search out stories that are newsworthy and topical.

It's important to understand the difference between a media release and an editorial, otherwise you'll fail with both. A media release should be newsworthy, and is used to provide information about a business development or event your business is involved with. Its purpose is to guide the media outlet as to how you want the story to be positioned. An editorial, on the other hand, represents your expert podiatry opinion on a particular foot issue that is currently relevant.

Submitting a media release or editorial used to mean you were sending it to a newspaper and magazine, however with the increasing number of news-based websites, blogs and social media sites this is quickly changing, and you need to be aware of this. Media releases and editorials build credibility and, best of all, they are free. Journalists and Editors look for media releases and editorials that their readership will find interesting, so make sure your submissions match the readership of the outlet you are submitting to.

Journalists become annoyed if you regularly bombard them with nonsense stories that are clearly nothing more than self-promotion or simply boring, so make sure your topics are newsworthy and interesting. Use the following list as a guide for creating media releases and editorials:

- **A business milestone**: Opening, expanding or relocating an existing business, winning an award, or celebrating a business anniversary are all business milestones that should be captured with a media release.

- **Doing something unique:** Preseason foot screenings at local sporting associations are always newsworthy, especially if it involves children.

- **Time/calendar specific:** Back to school is a perfect opportunity for an editorial focusing on the importance of proper fitting school shoes and general foot health.

- **A charity event:** Any event that is trying to raise money or raise awareness about a specific disorder or disease is a perfect opportunity for a media release, especially if it involves a charity walk or fun run.

- **A corporate challenge:** If your business is involved in a corporate challenge, use it to your advantage and contact the media.

- **Introduction of a new service**: If you introduce a new service that has not previously been available in your area and it is something that will benefit the community, this is newsworthy. Laser treatment for fungal nails is a perfect topic that could be used as both a media release and an editorial.

- **Celebrity news:** Commenting on celebrities has become commonplace on social media, however if it's a big story you should jump on it as soon as possible and contact your local newspapers. Serena Williams losing a match to an unknown player at the Australian Tennis Open because of sore feet is newsworthy. You could follow this media release with an editorial on foot injuries in tennis.

A media release should be no more than 250 words, and if it relates to an upcoming event it should be sent out several days beforehand so the Journalist involved has time to contact you for an interview. An editorial should be between 300 and 600 words. If you have photographs, send them, but more than likely they will send out a photographer for more professional shots. Always request copies of any photographs taken, as they may be useful for future marketing and can be posted online.

Other information you need to provide in your media release:

- When did it happen or when will it happen?

- Who does it involve?

- What is the significance or why is it newsworthy?

- Who is the best person to contact for comments?

- Where is the best place for a photo opportunity?

- Supply the best contact phone numbers.

You should find the names of your local Journalists and add their details to your address book. Send them an introductory email, letting them know who you are, your interests and where your business is located. After they reply, which they usually will, contact them via LinkedIn and add them as a business contact. Also, if you read an article written by a particular Journalist and you've sincerely enjoyed it, send them an email telling them so. This kind gesture will be remembered.

"Whoever controls the media, controls the mind."

Jim Morrison (The Doors)

TELEPHONE DIRECTORIES

Hard copy telephone directories are outdated, but some people do still use them. However, more and more people are using their online equivalent. In fact, I cannot remember the last time I actually picked up the phone book, which is why I now concentrate my efforts more on my online directory advertising, and I'm not alone. *Have you noticed how much smaller the telephone books have become?*

With all hard copy directories you need to know the closing date, which is the last date for booking an ad, and the publication date, which is when it will be released to the public. There is usually a three to four month gap between these two dates, and if you're opening a new business you need to get your timing right. Directory advertising has never been cheap, and the size of the ad will determine your costs and positioning in the directory. If your directory has a locality guide you should consider advertising in this section because some patients will look in this section of the directory as a quick reference to see if there is a Podiatrist in their area.

TELEVISION ADVERTISING

I've always been a huge fan of television advertising, because living in a regional area means it's relatively inexpensive and the costs vary depending on the time slot and length of the commercial. Television commercials will be either 15 or 30 seconds, and I am of the belief that if you can get your message across in 15 seconds then that's great, because it means you can place more ads (increased frequency) with the same budget.

There is one downside to television advertising though, and that is with more and more free-to-air channels, pay television, internet downloads and other technological distractions, it is becoming less and less effective, but it still does work, you just need to be more specific with ad placement. If you're considering television advertising, especially regionally, I've always preferred early morning, daytime and late evening because it's great value for money, which means you can advertise more often. Producing a television commercial is also not as expensive as you may think – a decent television commercial can be produced for under $800.

You may have noticed at the beginning and end of some television programs it says, *"This program has been brought to you by..."*, and it will mention a particular business. This quick message is called a *billboard* and they are free, but to receive free billboard advertising you need to run a minimum of three ads during the televised program. Billboards have fantastic impact, because many people will be in front of their televisions waiting for their program to start.

RADIO ADVERTISING

Once again, if you live in a regional area you'll find radio advertising inexpensive and quite effective because there are usually only a few commercial stations to choose from. The advantage radio advertising has over television is the low production costs and the speed at which a campaign can go to air, however there are some commonalities between television and radio advertising packages which you should be aware of.

With both you can purchase a package called ROS (run of station), which means you buy a specific number of commercials and they will be placed randomly throughout the month. ROS packages are cost effective, however you have no control over your advertising placement. As an alternative, both television and radio offer time-specific advertising, which means you request a specific time or program each day and you can select the particular days of the week as well. This form of advertising is more expensive, but can be far more effective in reaching your target markets. When I first began television and radio advertising I only purchased the ROS packages, however experience has taught me that both have their merits because ROS advertising offers frequency and time-specific advertising offers reach.

Radio though has a few more advertising options that television cannot match, such as live reads. A live read is when the host of the radio program reads an ad about your business during their program, usually lasting 30 to 60 seconds. If the host has a lot of credibility, it immediately gives your business credibility.

Another advertising option is a live broadcast from your business. The radio station basically sets up their radio hosts out the front of your business, and it can be combined with a sausage sizzle. I have done this a few times myself and they are a lot of fun, however it is never cheap, but it can be very effective if you've recently relocated your premises or if you have a retail arm to your podiatry business and you want to do a large promotion of new products.

All radio stations have a prize patrol van that zips around to different business locations, usually in the mornings, promoting products, services and free giveaways. The idea of the van is to have passing motorists stop to pick up a few freebies, while at the same time promoting the location of the business they are out the front of. Whenever you're negotiating a radio campaign, make sure the Sales Rep includes the prize patrol stopping at your business as part of the deal.

In your area there will more than likely be a talkback radio program. If so, contact them about doing a regular segment about podiatry. This is quite easy to organise leading up to Foot Health Month, however once your foot is in the door, enquire about doing a regular segment. If you can't get it for free, enquire how much it is to pay for a regular segment. I've been doing a regular radio segment in my local area for the past few years and it is very worthwhile.

SPONSORSHIP

I remember the first sporting team I sponsored, and it was exciting seeing my business name on the back of a team shirt, but was it really sponsorship or was it a donation so they could buy team shirts? It took me many years to understand that sponsorship needs to have commercial potential, which can be leveraged to attract new patients to your podiatry business. Sponsorship should be taken seriously, and all information about the sponsorship arrangement should be in a signed agreement, detailing what you are receiving for your sponsorship dollars. Are you being offered free tickets, signage opportunities, and will your business be mentioned in media releases? Will your logo be printed on all promotional materials, and are they putting a link on their website to your website or blog?

If you're sponsoring a club or community organisation you should insist on a copy of their membership list, and if you're sponsoring a specific event you should insist on a copy of their participants list. Having access to their database is far more important than all the offerings above because it gives you an opportunity to make further contact, via email, mail or both.

You need to understand the group you are sponsoring so you can target your message accordingly. If my business sponsors the local touch football competition, which runs all year round, my podiatry message to them would differ to participants training and competing in the Cairns Ironman. Even though the Ironman competitors are training all year round as well, they are building up to a specific event on a specific date, they are not competing week in, week out at the same level of intensity. Their training is different and so too are the types of foot and ankle concerns they may have before, during and after an event.

Sponsorship does not have to involve a cash transaction, instead your sponsorship may involve donating time to assist with the event, or you may offer prizes. Giving away prizes and not cash works very well at triathlons and various running events. As a Podiatrist, offering an initial biomechanical assessment is great because it costs you nothing other than the time it takes for you to complete an assessment. If you do offer an assessment as a prize, do up a gift voucher and make sure it is *only valid for one month*. This is really important because you want an instant short-term response from the event. This is even more important if you offer this prize regularly throughout the year. Only about half of the gift vouchers will ever be used before the expiry date.

Before you agree to any form of sponsorship you need to consider the following:

- Can I get a copy of their database?

- What is the real cost to my business? (Gift vouchers, your time or cash.)

- What publicity will my business receive?
    - Are they advertising this event on TV?

- o Are flyers being handed out prior to the event and on the day?

- o Can you put up signage for additional exposure?

- How many people will see your business name at the event?

  - o Be realistic. *If you're sponsoring a local under 10's basketball team that your son or daughter plays in, consider it a donation, not sponsorship.*

- Can I reach this many people with other advertising mediums? This is the most important question of all.

  - o If you put the same money, time and effort into another form of marketing, would you get a better return on your investment?

  - o Once again you need to be honest. *I know if I place a display ad in Saturday's newspaper I will get a profitable return, sometimes 10 times my investment. Will your sponsorship do the same?*

Always look for opportunities; don't wait for them to come to you. In your local area there will be many sporting and social events scheduled throughout the year that attract a lot of community attention and will attract the attention of many media outlets. Offering your services at these events will cost you nothing, but will give you a lot of exposure. Contact the organisers of these events and offer your services, free of charge, then let your media contacts know that you are the event Podiatrist. As the event draws closer, send media releases related to the upcoming event and how podiatry can benefit the participants.

If you're approached to sponsor an event and you notice the event has no major sponsor, enquire if you can have the naming rights, therefore taking ownership of the event. If it's successful, you should see if you're able to lock in a three- or five-year deal. My podiatry business was approached to sponsor the cheerleading squad for the Northern Pride Rugby League team in the Queensland Cup. It didn't happen, but during our negotiations it became apparent that Barlow the Lion, their mascot, was not sponsored, so we struck a deal that benefited both parties and when the 2014 season concludes we will determine if we should pursue a similar deal for 2015 and beyond.

Alternatively, it's not hard to create your own event if you're already involved in a particular sport and you know all the right people. For example, at every grand final – whether it is for rugby, soccer, hockey or whatever – there will be little to no entertainment at the half-time break, therefore enquire about having an annual "Dash for Cash", which could be a team or individual event. Because there will be hundreds of people at the grand final, your expenditure will be eclipsed by your exposure. Once again you should be able to turn this event into a newsworthy media release, especially if it can become an annual event.

> "You can't manufacture emotion. It's already there.
> When you find it - just find a way to trigger it; tap into it;
> fuel it; and watch it grow into something remarkable."
>
> Mark Harrison (Chair of the Canadian Sponsorship Forum)

As you can see, external marketing is extensive and there is a lot of crossover and linkages between various forms of external marketing. Sponsorship can link quite easily with a media release or editorial, and you can easily link a newspaper ad with your radio and television campaign. Remember, your goal with external marketing is to attract your target market to your podiatry business, and then use your internal marketing to win them over and make them fans of your business.

*After reading this chapter, what ideas are going through your head? Write them down **right now**.*

_____

_____

_____

_____

_____

_____

_____

_____

26

MARKETING PILLAR FIVE: VERBAL MARKETING

I look at verbal marketing as any form of marketing that involves you opening your mouth and talking. If you get nervous meeting people for the first time or talking in front of crowds, don't be concerned – it's normal and you're not alone. I read an article once on people's fears, and public speaking was right at the top of the list, just in front of death by fire. In New Zealand it was second behind snakes…and there are no snakes in New Zealand, so figure that one out.

> "There are only two types of speakers in the world. The nervous and the liars."
>
> Mark Twain

In this chapter I will discuss the most common forms of community marketing and a few tips of how you can get the most out of them.

NETWORKING

I've always enjoyed networking and meeting like-minded business people who openly share their thoughts and ideas with no hidden agendas. I enjoy hearing positive news about their businesses, because as business people we're bombarded with negative energy on a daily basis and I think this is even more applicable in the health industry. Negative energy, day after day, can take its toll on your attitude so networking is a fantastic opportunity to get away from your podiatry business and take a dose of positive energy from people outside of our industry.

On the surface, the concept of networking is very simple. The goal is to link like-minded individuals who have a common interest together, and through relationship building and trust they become walking, talking advertisements for one another's businesses. For networking to be effective you must be genuine and honest and look at networking with a long-term view. You need to build trust with the person you're talking to. Never treat networking as a one-way promotional activity for yourself and your business. This is a networking killer. People you meet will see right through you if your only purpose in talking to them is to shove your podiatry business down their throat. Don't become *"that person"* – the one everybody in the room wants to avoid. People you meet at networking events will only refer people they know once the relationship between you is nourished and you have built trust. The best part of networking is it's one of the least expensive marketing activities you will undertake.

Some networking events are free, however others may cost you the price of a nice lunch, which if you compare this to other forms of advertising is very cheap. Podiatrists will drop $450 on a display ad in a newspaper, but will hesitate paying $45 to attend a networking event. I still find networking one of the most cost-effective business strategies for my podiatry business.

Not all networking events or groups are business orientated; some are community organisations such as Rotary, Lions and Apex. I was a member of Rotary for a few years and it was a great experience. I met some great people who are still close friends. Even though my membership lapsed I can still be involved via charity golf days and other social events, which keeps me in the minds of the membership and also makes me first choice to organise speaking engagements during Foot Health Month. *How many Rotary Clubs are in your area?*

So where do you find networking groups? First you need to open your eyes and read the local newspaper. Most business organisations and other groups will have a regular networking meeting. Here are a few examples of state and national organisations that will have a presence in your local area for sure:

- Chamber of Commerce

- Australian Institute of Management (AIM)

- Rotary

- Lions Club.

Another type of organisation you should not overlook is the Business Women's Clubs in your area – they are amazing organisations. Yes...if you're male you can still attend, which I have done on numerous occasions with my wife Christine, and when there are 200-plus females and only a handful of males, you are going to be noticed. *You may even get lucky.* A good friend of mine, Scott Brown, from allsigns print and design, is a networking master, and each year he organises a men's table at the Business Womens Annual Christmas lunch. Are we noticed? Yes we are!

Some business organisations will also have networking tables, and if they do, it's always beneficial to provide some form of flyer or clinic information brochures if you have them available. It's important to remember that when you're attending a networking function you are representing your podiatry business; therefore you must always conduct yourself in a professional manner.

Opportunities for networking are only limited by your thinking. If there's no allied health networking group in your area, start one. Write to local Physiotherapists, Osteopaths, Chiropractors and Dieticians and try to get them to a meeting, before or after work, even if it is just at a local coffee shop. If you only have four people attend the first meeting then that's four opportunities to create long-term relationships. *If you're the person organising the new networking group, you don't have to invite other Podiatrists. Let them find out about it through the network.*

PROMOTIONAL ITEMS

To assist in promoting your podiatry business further you may want to have some promotional items available that can be handed out at networking and other events. Promotional items can also be used with your internal marketing. I'm sure you will have a company in your area that produces promotional items, but always check the quality of their work as you don't want to hand out poor-quality items. Common promotional items include coffee mugs, pens, t-shirts, caps, golf balls and water bottles. The initial outlay can sometimes be quite expensive, however promotional products can be very effective when used wisely and can make you look far bigger than you actually are. It is important to remember that these items give the receiver an impression of you and your business, so always go for quality over quantity.

> "I've learned that people will forget what you
> said, people will forget what you did, but people
> will never forget how you made them feel."
>
> Maya Angelou

DON'T HAND OUT YOUR BUSINESS CARDS

I remember the excitement I felt when I was handed my first business card. It made all the years at university seem worthwhile. I also couldn't wait to show my family and friends and start handing them out, however have you ever considered how many of your business cards go from the person's wallet to their rubbish bin within the first 48 hours? I would hazard a guess and say most of them, especially if you forced your business card on someone who didn't ask for it.

You should make people want your business card, but what does that really mean? Well, if you're at a networking event and someone says they have a sore foot, before rushing in with your business card, as you normally would, stop for a moment and ask a few questions about their particular foot ailment. After they have given you more information, explain how many times you've successfully treated this particular condition. Then ask how serious are they about fixing their current problem. If they say that they want it fixed as soon as possible, tell them that you can probably get them an appointment later in the week if you move a few things around, then present your business card to them – but never go past half of the distance between them and you. If they want your business card they will come the other half and take the card from you.

But...here's an alternative idea if you're brave...You're at a networking event and someone says they have a foot problem and asks for your business card. Once again, don't give them your card; instead ask them for more information about their foot problem, then take out two business cards. But, instead of giving them one, ask for their mobile telephone number. As they give you their number, write it on one business card, and on the back of the other business card write a date and a time and say, "*I'm going to*

197

call you tomorrow at 12.30 pm, during my lunch break, to make an appointment for you. Is that okay?" If they say that would be great then they're serious about wanting an appointment, but if they hesitate and say, *"No it's okay, I'll call you"*, then they're wasting your time. Move on and talk to someone else!

PUBLIC SPEAKING OPPORTUNITIES

My first public speaking engagement was for Sports Medicine Australia in front of 10 unfortunate people – and I say unfortunate because it was nothing short of abysmal. It was so bad the Doctor who organised the talk asked me to promise to never speak in public again, and he wasn't joking. I'll admit, my confidence was low, but then I realised I could only get better, and I did. I went from abysmal to terrible, from terrible to bad, and so on.

If you have a fear of public speaking, as I did, you need to deal with it, because public speaking opens so many doors that are otherwise closed off to you. Joining Toastmasters or a similar group may be able to assist you with public speaking, but for me I just threw myself in the deep end and decided I needed to sink or swim – and unfortunately I sank, but I learnt the more I did it the better I got because *everything is hard, until it's easy.*

Now I can talk to any size group, and I've learnt that being a little nervous before a talk or presentation is a good thing. It means you still care about the subject and your audience sees your nerves as excitement. The adrenaline hit you get after a public speaking engagement can be addictive, but it's a great addiction to have and there are many long-term benefits of becoming more engaged through public speaking:

- You will come across as a *perceived expert: remember, perception is reality.*

- If you are an *expert* then the podiatry business you own and operate must also be exceptional.

- Speaking to groups of people at one time is a great way to leverage your time and promote your business for free.

- THIS IS MY FAVOURITE: Every time you say yes to a speaking opportunity, it's one less speaking opportunity for your competitors. If you don't do it, they will.

Here is a brief overview of some of the organisations that you should approach about giving a podiatry presentation, but *always keep in mind your target market. If it doesn't fit, say no*:

- Rotary, Lions and Apex

- sports stores – this also improves your non-professional referrals

- Independent Retirees' Association

- primary school health days

- sporting clubs (coaches and managers, pre-season club meetings)

- gyms (during staff meetings)

- professional service businesses (accounting and law offices)

- local physiotherapy and doctors' groups – further increases your professional referrals

- Falls Prevention Society

- Diabetes Australia.

HAVING A BOOTH AT LOCAL SHOWS AND TRADE EXPOS

Having a booth at local shows and trade expos provides great opportunities to promote your business and the services you provide to large numbers of people in a very short period of time, however if you have a booth, make sure it looks professional, and you must make sure it is always staffed. There's nothing worse than seeing an empty booth – it does not give a good image.

Also be prepared to do a lot of talking, which is why I have placed this in verbal marketing. Yes, having a booth could also be classed as external marketing, but this is the thing with marketing pillars, they are no hard-and-fast rules. Most local shows and trade expos will attract a lot of tyre kickers, so your primary goal is to collect names and email addresses via competitions or free offers for more information, and then let your marketing systems sift through them and sort the good from the bad.

DO YOU HAVE AN ELEVATOR SPEECH?

What *is* an elevator speech? An elevator speech is a concise, informative, compelling summary of who you are and what you do. Your speech needs to be told in 30 to 60 seconds, the same amount of time it takes for you to go from the ground floor to the tenth level in an elevator.

This may sound trivial, but there are many occasions when you meet someone and they ask what you do and you know you only have a brief moment to explain yourself. By the time you "um 'n' ah" the opportunity may be lost. Therefore you need to be able to communicate what you do very quickly, and you need to practise this technique.

Elevator speeches are also handy to have at networking and lunch meetings, because you meet a lot of people in a short space of time. This happens rarely, but sometimes I've been at lunch meetings and the MC of the event will ask if anyone would like to stand up or come on stage for one or two minutes to talk briefly about their business...it's at these times when an elevator speech is needed.

With all verbal marketing, it all comes back to you having the ability to talk and communicate with other people. If you don't have the skill, learn it, otherwise you're gifting work and your share of the podiatry wealth pie to your competition.

Remember: *It's No Secret, There's Money In Podiatry, however...* you must overcome your fears.

*After reading this chapter, what ideas are going through your head? Write them down **right now**.*

_____

_____

_____

_____

_____

_____

_____

_____

MARKETING PILLAR SIX: WEB-BASED MARKETING

Web-based marketing is more than having a simple website about your business, though some businesses don't even have that. On a recent webinar presented by Andrew Griffiths, he said a staggering 53% of small businesses still do not have a website. I find this surprising, however don't 50% of small business also go broke in the first two to five years? Maybe there's a correlation here...I don't know the exact statistics for the entire podiatry profession, but in Cairns 41% of podiatrists have a website, 18% have websites under construction and they've been that way for some time, and 41% do not have a website at all.

Web-based marketing is cost effective and is a great way to advertise – $5000 spent on television or radio advertising can be gone within a month, however put that same budget to work with web-based marketing and you could be reaping the rewards a year later. There is a plethora of web-based marketing ideas, which is why there are whole books written on the subject. My goal in this chapter is to give you the basics and to get you thinking about it more often. If you're already a web-based marketing king or queen I congratulate you, because you've seen what others have failed to see.

This is a fast-changing area, so it's vital that you stay up to date. I've always been a fan of technology, but even I had my eyes opened recently at a Top Practices Summit in Nashville, where Tom Foster and Danielle Ruderman from Foster Web Marketing discussed, in depth, the sweeping changes that have been taking place with Google and how websites are ranked based on content, keywords and other factors.

THE WEBSITE

First things first: you need to have a quality website. From the outset it needs to be visually appealing and easy to navigate. It needs regular content added because you want people coming back to your website as a reference source, and once they are there you want them to stay for as long as possible because the longer they stay on your website and the more pages they navigate through, the better Google will rank your website. Therefore you need a website developer who understands this and will keep you informed as changes occur. Fortunately for me, in addition to my website developers I have a good friend in Cairns, Nicky Jurd, who is the author of *REFRESH...How to Make Your Website More Awesome and Less Stinky*, and over our weekly coffee meetings she keeps me informed about consumer trends and other web-based changes to be aware of.

If you designed your own website, be careful, because even ugly kids look good to their parents. Your website represents you and your podiatry business, which is why you should use a professional website developer. They can improve your graphics and links, and assist with content and search engine optimisation, meaning you're found more often. Your website should be constantly improving; it's not something you just do once and then never come back to again, though unfortunately this *is* what many

Podiatrists do. They will eagerly have a website created and maybe tweak it a few times in the first month, then forget about it.

If you haven't changed your website for some time, make an appointment to see your website developer and discuss what changes are needed to get it up to date. Also make sure it is responsive so it can be viewed on both smart phones and tablets, because more and more people are using these devices and not traditional laptops and desktops to search for information. The statistics are staggering and between 30% and 50% of website visitors now come from a mobile device.

When your website is firing on all cylinders you'll notice an increase in traffic and patient enquiries, but never rest; constantly go back to your website and look at it as though you're a patient, because techno glitches can happen. I receive weekly emails from my website developers reminding me to add content to my editorials, my FAQ and my blog. I also have quarterly coaching sessions with my website developers, which is extremely helpful.

Google Analytics is also a feature you need grasp and understand. It basically gives you detailed statistics about web traffic to and from your website, and it also lets you know what search engines were used to find your site, how long people stayed on each particular page, whether they clicked through to another page, and if so what pages were most popular, or did they leave your site after the first click? This information is important to have because it informs you about what pages are working, which are not, and if you need to make changes. Your web developer will probably be able to help you with all this. If not, it's time to start shopping for a new developer.

COLLECTING EMAILS VIA YOUR WEBSITE

Your website should have an area where people can ask questions and request free information. You've probably seen this on other websites, where it says *click here* to receive our free report or our free e-book. When you do this, not only do you receive what you requested but you also receive ongoing newsletters and campaign flyers until you unsubscribe. If you're enjoying the content and information provided you'll stay subscribed, and this is their goal. They want to stay in regular contact with people until they're ready to buy. Your website needs to be set up in a similar fashion.

You then need to be able to collect all the names and email addresses using a CRM (customer relationship management) program so your business can stay in regular contact with people until they're ready to become a patient. Some website developers have their own CRM program that automatically enters these names for you directly from your website, however if this service is not available you need to purchase a CRM program separately and enter the names and email address manually. There are also free CRM programs available if you search online. You should also add the names and email addresses collected at shows and expos to your CRM program.

Over time you will add your existing patients to the same CRM program, but they are contacted in a different way and with different information. All names and email addresses when put together become a very powerful marketing database, and that holds huge value for your business when it comes time to selling, but until then it gives you a bigger share of the podiatry market.

YOUR BLOG

You need a least one blog and this should be attached to your website, however you can have a secondary blog as well using Blogger for example, which is owned by Google, but there are many other companies offering free blog hosting. Do a simple search online and you'll see what I mean. A blog is usually written by one person, however if you're in a group practice your website blog may have multiple contributors and it should be updated regularly. Most blogs will centre on one specific topic, so in this case your blog would centre on your podiatry business and the services it offers.

This is why you may consider a secondary or even a third blog. If you have a strong interest in treating foot problems associated with triathletes then this would be an ideal blog opportunity. Your goal with blogging is to develop followers and to create word-of-mouth marketing. You want followers telling their friends about your blog, so always be informative, but make sure your blog is focused on your reader, not on your ego or opinion. If someone leaves a comment on your blog, be responsive.

VIDEO CONTENT

Do you need video content on your website? Yes, you do. Go online and look at the statistical data; it's mind blowing. Video is both educational and entertaining, and people will recall information they've seen on video long after viewing it, yet they will forget what they've read within days. Your website therefore needs to have video content added, ideally on each page, even if it's just a simple 30-second introductory video about the content on the page.

How should your patients stretch their hamstrings? How do you strap your ankles before sport? How do you test the stability of running shoes? These questions, and more, can all be answered by recording instructional videos, and they need to be added to your website. You can have your video content recorded by a professional, and if I was shooting a television commercial this is exactly what I would do, however an iPhone 5 has HD recording capabilities and – as long as your lighting and sound are good – there's no reason why you cannot shoot your own 30-second videos for most pages on your website. Just get yourself a stable platform or tripod so you don't shoot another Blair Witch Project.

Any instructional videos you create should also be loaded onto **YouTube**, **Vimeo** and other sites such as **Facebook** and **Google+**, because this will help you with your online presence in the social media world and drive more people back to your website. There are many video-sharing websites, but it's better to focus on the main ones and do it right rather than try to load video on every available site and do it poorly.

FACEBOOK AND GOOGLE+ BUSINESS PAGES

At the start of this chapter I discussed how many Podiatrists in Cairns had a website and it was 41%. So, how many do you think would have a have a Facebook page for their business? The answer is 33% and excluding my own, which I update weekly, the most recently updated one was early 2012, about two years ago. When I search Google+ it was even worse, only 25% had an online Google+ presence and there was no content added on any of them.

Is it any wonder why some podiatry businesses prosper while others struggle? Online Marketing for your podiatry business via social networking is something you need to do because you can communicate and reach so many people in such a short period of time. Early this year (2014), I posted an article on our business Facebook page and within 48 hours it had reached over 1700 people...and it cost us nothing.

Even though **Facebook** and **Google** dominate the social networking scene right now, don't discount the importance of having your business details on **Yahoo**, **Bing** and **Yelp**, because people search in different ways and things change quickly, therefore you should also have **Twitter** and **Pinterest** accounts. What is interesting about Yelp is every review added is also linked to Yellow Pages Online advertising. It is for this reason you need patients to be adding good reviews about your business on as many social websites as possible. **WOMO**, Word Of Mouth Online, is a new-comer on the social scene and is also worth looking at. It's only new and it could be huge, or gone in a few years' time.

ONLINE DIRECTORIES

I read an interesting statistic recently that said 85% of all purchases begin with an online search, and the most common way to search is using an online directory such as Yellow Pages Online. When a person uses an online directory they are more inclined to make a purchase compared to when they do a general search on Google, Yahoo, Bing or Yelp for example, because they have a better idea of what it is they want when they go to the directory.

I think online directories are popular because we grew up using the paper versions for so many years so we still feel comfortable using them. For this reason you need to make sure your online information is correct and up to date each year. Another improvement in recent years with online directories is the ability to be able to edit online content ourselves, so as changes occur throughout the year you can make an immediate change. The more content, video, photos, brochures and downloadable information you can add to your online directory, the more it will rise in the online rankings.

SUMMARY

This is by no means a complete list of everything that needs attention when it comes to web-based marketing but it's a good starting point, and if you've not given it much thought now is the time to get started. This book is all about making money in podiatry, and even though this is one of the last chapters of the book this should really be one of the first things you get organised, because it costs you nothing to get started. I'll be really interested to read this chapter again in five years to see what has changed. Do Facebook and Google still dominate or is there a new player in the market? Is there something we have not even heard of yet...I think there will be.

I've mentioned numerous times that my podiatry business is busier today than it's ever been and we're constantly having record sales month after month, and I don't think it's because I'm special in anyway – it's because I'm not lazy. Some of this web-based marketing stuff is very simple, and in all honesty it only takes a few hours each week to get it organised. If you cannot afford a few hours then outsource this task to someone else, but either way it needs to get done.

To get the best results from your marketing you need to work on all six Marketing Pillars, not just one or two, or the ones you feel comfortable with – you need to work on all of them simultaneously. Individually each pillar is good; but together they are great.

Remember: *It's No Secret, There's Money In Podiatry,* however... you need to have a huge online footprint.

> *After reading this chapter, what ideas are going through your head? Write them down* **right now***.*
>
> _____
>
> _____
>
> _____
>
> _____
>
> _____
>
> _____

28
CREATE YEARLY MARKETING FOLDERS

In 1994 I started keeping copies of all my advertising and marketing – and I mean *everything*. Not just ads placed in the newspaper, but copies of editorials, brochures, newsletters and even a copy of my business card at that time. As this information grew, I decided I had to keep it in some sort of orderly fashion and so began the process of creating *Marketing Folders* each year. I'm glad I did this because looking on my bookshelf and seeing 20 years of past advertising and marketing shows me how far my business has grown. I still look through these folders on a regular basis for inspiration.

You should start your marketing folder as soon as possible and keep it up to date. Marketing items should be added in chronological order, and it's best to divide the folder into monthly sections. When you add an item, attach handwritten notes, especially if there was something unique you want to remember about this particular item in the future. If your folder is full before the end of the year, it means you're keeping busy.

You could use your computer to scan and save all your marketing activities instead of using a folder, and I did do this for a short period of time myself, but it doesn't have the same impact as seeing your marketing folders grow, year by year, along your bookshelf. Hard copy folders are also easier to review. If business ever slows, immediately turn to your marketing folder. Is it full or is it looking a little thin?

Here is a list of what needs to be included in your marketing folder:

- Television and radio schedules: *Your Sales Rep will provide you with schedules before the month commences.*

- Newspaper advertisements: *Record the page number, the date and the day of publication. Also note down if the weather was poor. Bad weather does affect outcomes.*

- Media releases: *As above with newspapers.*

- Phone directories: *These directories are outdated, however if you do advertise in them put a copy in your folder. Make sure it is added in the month the book was distributed.*

- Online directories: *Once again, add a copy to the month it became live, and add additional copies if it is changed in any way during the contract period.*

- Other online marketing: *As above with online directories.*

- Note any changes to your website: *If you update, edit or add new pages to your website, make a copy and add it to your marketing folder.*

- Copies of all printed materials: *A copy of all brochures and flyers, as well as details regarding distribution areas and quantity.*

- Sponsorship information: *If you sponsor a team or individual, add a copy of your agreement, and when it comes to a conclusion, record your thoughts regarding the positives and negatives of this sponsorship arrangement and if you would do it again.*

- Networking and business functions: *After every networking event, you should note who you met and what you learnt from the evening. Also, was it a worthwhile function and would you attend again?*

- Community talks and presentations: *Once again, note what went well and what you would change. Record the organiser's contact details for future reference.*

- Patient letters: *Every standard letter you use for recalling patients or reactivating patients should be added in the month it was created. Every time you make a change, no matter how small, a new copy should be added.*

- Professional referrer's letters: *As above with patient letters. For simplicity, I now use a separate folder to store all my outgoing letters so they don't get lost among my other marketing activities.*

- Professional referrer personal visits: *Every meeting with a professional referrer should be recorded and also your feelings about the meeting.*

- Email marketing: *If you do a group email to your patients, professional referrers or anyone else, make sure you keep a copy. I like to keep a copy of my emails in the same folder as my letters. (This also includes email newsletters.)*

- Information evenings: *You should note down the topic for the evening, a list of everyone invited, how many RSVPs were received, and who did not attend.*

If you're unsure if an item should go into your marketing folder then it probably should because it can always be removed at a later date.

Regardless of how well you track your marketing, the quote below by John Wanamaker (1838–1922) is important to remember.

> **"Half my advertising is wasted, I just don't know which half."**

This quote has stood the test of time and is still talked about today, because when John Wanamaker died he had a net worth of over a billion dollars in today's money, and he did this knowing that only half his advertising worked. With the technology and knowledge we have today, we have the ability to be far more accurate in determining the effectiveness of our marketing, however you need to be diligent and you need to care. Many Podiatrists don't care, have no marketing plans in place, and have kept little to no records of their past marketing activities, so they may as well be living in the 1800s.

MONTHLY REFERRAL SOURCES

Every new patient should be asked how he or she heard about your podiatry business, and this information needs to be as accurate as possible. Regardless of what a patient writes on their patient information sheet, I will still enquire a little further because I want accurate information. If they write WOM – word of mouth – this is too vague; you need to ask more questions.

You should print your "referral sources" each month and add this information to your yearly marketing folder. You should see patterns developing between your monthly referrals and your ongoing marketing activities. You will be surprised where your referrals come from, which is why it is important to record all your marketing activities, not just the ones you think are important.

YEARLY CALENDAR FOR NEXT YEAR

At the end of each year I like to set one day aside and reflect on the previous year's marketing activities. I find this process very therapeutic and enjoyable, and it can be a rewarding exercise to do with other team members, especially if they have been involved in the thought process. If time permits, go back and look at the past five years, and after reviewing these folders, use this information to develop your marketing plan for the next 12 months.

As each year passes you'll notice successful marketing ideas will be repeated, especially your Black Caviars, which makes planning for the upcoming year much easier. It's also important to evaluate your marketing ideas that did not quite hit the mark and try to learn from them so you do not repeat the same mistake twice.

An interesting story I would like to share is how I made the decision in 1994 to start keeping a record of all my advertising. At the beginning of that year a small-minded Podiatrist reported me to the Registration Board about breeching advertising rules, and as part of his complaint he provided them with copies of all my advertising for the previous 12 months. Of course he was proven to be wrong by the Registration Board, but I was really impressed seeing all my advertising for the past

12 months presented in such an organised format, so I borrowed the idea and have been using it ever since!

It's No Secret, There's No Money In Podiatry...but you must reflect on the past, learn from the present and plan for the future.

*After reading this chapter, what ideas are going through your head? Write them down **right now**.*

_____

_____

_____

_____

_____

_____

_____

CONCLUSION

Take a close look at our profession and you'll realise that there are some Podiatrists making some ridiculous amounts of money, which is why *It's No Secret, There's Money In Podiatry*. However, for you to achieve this, you must first believe it is truly possible. Without belief you have nothing.

I attended a business seminar in 1998 with about 100 other people, and the speaker asked everyone to write down how much money they would like to earn in the next financial year. He then asked everyone to write down all the things they needed to change in their personal and work life to make this income goal a reality. He explained how we only needed to make minor changes in our thinking and in our actions to make this goal a reality, which made perfect sense.

Then, just as I was getting comfortable with my new income goal, he said, okay, now I want you to triple it. The room exploded, and my initial thought was, *"You're kidding me aren't you?"* But as he continued to talk I understood the point he was trying to make. To achieve a small goal, a goal just out of your reach, you only need to make small changes, but to achieve a much bigger goal, such as tripling your income in 12 months, you would have to make much bigger changes, and in some cases massive changes.

You need to understand how your mind works. Small goals will not push you mentally, because you already know they can be achieved with little or no additional effort, however larger goals require you to think and act vastly differently. To achieve a goal like tripling your income, you must first believe you can do it, and once you believe it is a possibility only then will you take all the necessary steps required for its attainment.

Someone asked me why I would want to write a book about establishing a successful podiatry business, and I had two really simple answers:

1. It wasn't written when I graduated in 1989, and I wish it had been because it would have saved me a lot of time and money. In 2013 it still hadn't been written, so it was definitely time.

2. Whenever I attended a podiatry conference I would always have Podiatrists asking me questions and picking my brain about business, so instead of telling them the same things each time, I thought, let's get these ideas down on paper. So now I can say to them *buy my book,* instead of *buy me a beer and let's chat.*

For those of you who have purchased this book, I do hope you've enjoyed it, and I would love any feedback you may have and would also love to hear some of your success stories along the way, so when you can, please email me at tf@tysonfranklin.com. But always remember one really important thing, and I think Walt Disney said it best:

> *"A man (or woman) should never neglect his family for business."*

SO WHAT DOES A SMART PODIATRIST DO NEXT?

Right now could be the moment where you change your life forever, or it could be a moment that simply passes you by and is forgotten: the decision is yours. If you're feeling motivated you need to take action immediately. Don't wait until tomorrow, or next week, instead head straight to Tyson Franklin's website and register for his FREE newsletter: www.tysonfranklin.com.

Every month Tyson's newsletter will give you tips and ideas you can use immediately in your podiatry business that will generate instant profits. If you are not yet in business for yourself but you're thinking about it, register anyway for future reference; you won't be disappointed.

When you're ready, you can also attend one of Tyson's workshops. A list of upcoming topics and dates can be found on his website. If you do attend, be prepared to learn and have fun, because Tyson is not a boring speaker; he will keep you entertained all day, and before you realise you'll walk away fully charged and motivated to achieve more than you ever thought possible.

Tyson is also available to mentor a limited number of one-on-one clients, however this option is only available if you are serious about wanting to build an awesome podiatry business that stands out from the crowd. However, Tyson recommends you attend one of his workshops first, so you can see if you "click".

**"Sometimes if you want to see change for the better,
you have to take things into your own hands."**

Clint Eastwood